Multilateral Conferences and Diplomacy

D1740585

A Glossary of Terms for UN Delegates

Main contributors

Ronald A. Walker
Brook Boyer

United Nations Insitute for Training and Research

ISBN: 92-9182-036-8

Published by the United Nations Institute for Training and Research (UNITAR)

Cover design by [twice 2]

Printed in Switzerland by srokundig

Front cover - photo credit (left):
UNFCCC COP 6 plenary session by courtesy of Leila Mead/IISD

The opinions expressed in this glossary are those of the contributors and do not necessarily reflect the views of UNITAR, any of the other United Nations organs, bodies and agencies, or other organizations. This general disclaimer applies to the definitions of all the terms contained in the glossary.

The designation employed and the presentation of material in this publication do not imply the expression of any opinion whatsoever on the part of the United Nations Institute for Training and Research (UNITAR) concerning the legal status of any country, territory, city or area or its authorities, or concerning the delimitation of its frontiers and boundaries.

Material in this publication may be freely quoted but acknowledgement is requested, together with a reference to the document number. A copy of the publication containing the quotation or reprint should be sent to the United Nations Institute for Training and Research (UNITAR), Palais des Nations, CH-1211 Geneva 10, Switzerland.

► Preface

The United Nations, through its Headquarters in New York and Offices at Geneva, Vienna and Nairobi, convenes thousands of formal and informal, official and unofficial, meetings and conferences each year. Many events are recurring, such as the sessions of the General Assembly and the Economic and Social Council. The specialized agencies and other bodies and programmes hold hundreds of additional conferences, not to mention expert meetings, negotiation committees, working groups, and the growing number of conferences of the parties and subsidiary body meetings to major conventions.

Taken together, more than 10,000 meetings and conferences take place annually which involve the participation of diplomats from missions accredited to the United Nations, senior and ministerial officials and technical experts from capitals, and observers from intergovernmental and non-governmental organizations. Effective participation at these meetings and conferences requires delegates to master not only the substantive issues under discussion and debate, but also a rich vocabulary of terms specific to multilateral conferences organized in the context of the UN system.

This glossary provides definitions to over 700 terms, abbreviations and acronyms frequently heard at UN conferences. These terms relate to the structure and functioning of the United Nations organs, programmes and bodies, as well as the specialized agencies; regional intergovernmental organizations; decision-making processes, procedures and forums; regional and geographical groups; other groups and alliances; informal contact groups; and documents. The glossary also includes the names of many commonly mentioned international conferences and conventions. Terms are cross-referenced to enable users to identify similar terms and/or variations in the definition of a term.

The glossary is not an official document, and the list of terms is certainly not exhaustive. The glossary will hopefully complement other glossaries and dictionaries which have been published on diplomacy and international relations over the years, in addition to those published or disseminated by other organizations in the UN system.

The glossary targets primarily the newly accredited multilateral delegate who is unfamiliar with the wide array of UN-related terms and abbreviations, although it will no doubt be of equal assistance to other delegates, including scientific and technical experts from capitals, staff of the United Nations and other intergovernmental organizations, and representatives from non-governmental organizations.

Many individuals have contributed to the glossary's drafting, revision and editing. I wish to acknowledge in particular the glossary's two principal contributors: Ronald A. Walker, Visiting Fellow, Asia Pacific School of Diplomacy, Australian National University, and former Ambassador and Permanent Representative of Australia to the United Nations; and Brook Boyer, Senior Programme Officer of UNITAR. Other individuals who have contributed to earlier drafts, provided insightful comments and direction and/or provided editorial assistance include Isabel Hubert, Jean Gazarian, Rabih Haddad, Arun Seetulsingh, Birgit Viohl, Fabian Lemmes, Beat Kube, Chungwon Park, Hyun-Binn Cho and Frédéric M-Deschenes.

UNITAR is grateful to His Majesty Sultan Qaboos bin Said Al-Said for providing the Government of the Sultanate of Oman's support, without which the production and dissemination of this document would not be feasible.

Marcel A. Boisard
Assistant Secretary-General
Executive Director, UNITAR

▶ **User Notes**

This glossary aims to clarify a wide range of terms used in multilateral meetings and conferences. The definitions provided reflect current usage, which is not necessarily consistent from one organization or context to another. Some terms may also have an everyday meaning not given here, and some have particular meanings in international law, which the glossary does not purport to cover in detail.

Terms are also consistently evolving and many have no authoritative definition. The term "friend of the chair", for example, has been used for many decades to designate a delegate who has been charged by the presiding officer of a conference to perform a particular task (usually to find consensus on a body of issues). In the early to mid-1990s, some conferences have started to use the plural form of the term (e.g. friends of the chair) to designate members of a contact group convened by the presiding officer. Situations of this kind may cause confusion.

- ✓ Some terms have multiple definitions. They are provided in sequence (1, 2, 3…) with no order of importance;
- ✓ Words, abbreviations or acronyms in parentheses at the beginning of a definition indicate the context in which this usage is likely to be met;
- ✓ Terms in **bold** print are defined elsewhere in the glossary;
- ✓ Where relevant, World Wide Web page addresses are provided;
- ✓ Capitalization and spelling are according to the United Nations Editorial Manual (Department of Conference Services, New York, 1983). In general, capitals are only used for proper nouns (e.g. the name of a specific treaty, organization, etc.) or when the term is contextualised.

A

Aarhus Convention

Shorthand for the Convention on Access to Information, Public Participation in Decision-making, and Access to Justice in Environmental Matters, negotiated under the auspices of **UNECE**, adopted in Aarhus, Denmark and entered into force in 2001.

Abdus Salam ICTP

Abdus Salam International Centre for Theoretical Physics, legally referred to as 'International Centre for Theoretical Physics', is operated as a joint programme by **UNESCO** and **IAEA**. Administration is by UNESCO.

absent (from a vote)

Said of a **delegation** that does not **cast a vote**. It may be in the room but either not entitled, or choosing not, to vote.

ABS

(CBD) Access to genetic resources and benefit-sharing.

abstain (verb), abstention (noun)

To vote (or a vote that is) neither in favour nor against the question. It registers absence of support, but with less opposition than with a negative vote. Under most **rules of procedure**, **delegations** that abstain are not counted as 'present and voting' in that vote.

ACABQ

(GA) Advisory Committee on Administrative and Budgetary Questions. Members are appointed individually on the recommendation of the **Fifth Committee**.

acclamation

A procedure whereby a conference adopts a proposal without a **vote**, all **delegations** having indicated their support for it, e.g. by applause.

accreditation

The process of submitting credentials:
1. by representatives of a State, to an international organization;
2. by **delegates** (including observers), to an international conference.

ACP

African, Caribbean and Pacific Group. See **Cotonou Agreement**, **EPA** and **Lomé Conventions**.

www.acpsec.org

ACT

Amazon Cooperation Treaty adopted in 1978. See **ACTO**.

ACTO

Amazon Cooperation Treaty Organization. Established in 2002 as the **Secretariat** of the Amazon Cooperation Treaty among the Governments of Bolivia, Brazil, Colombia, Ecuador, Guyana, Peru, Suriname and Venezuela with the goal of promoting sustainable development in the Amazon.

www.octa.org.br/

Acts, the

(UPU) The Constitution of the **Universal Postal Union** and its six Additional Protocols.

ad hoc committee, ad hoc conference

A committee formed to deal with a particular topic, e.g. Ad Hoc Committee of the **GA** or of the **CD**. As applied to committees, the adjective is today only historical; its former inference that the committee was established on a temporary basis no longer applies. In the case of a conference, however, the term indicates that it is not part of an ongoing series and has been set up to perform a particular task.

ad referendum

Subject to subsequent agreement by government(s) *(Latin)*.

ADB

Asian Development Bank. One of the **regional development banks**. The same initials are sometimes used for the African Development Bank (**AfDB**).

www.adb.org

AfDB

African Development Bank. One of the **regional development banks**.

www.afdb.org

African Group

An **electoral group** in the **GA** and in most **specialized agencies** which also functions as a **caucus group** and coalition at many conferences. It is composed of all States in Africa, including the island States of the Eastern Atlantic Ocean and Western Indian Ocean and operates as a **sub-group** within the **G77**.

African Union (AU)

The principal and supreme regional organization in Africa, and successor organization to the former Organization of African Unity (OAU). All members of the **African Group** are members of the African Union, with the exception of Morocco.

www.africa-union.org

AFTA

ASEAN Free Trade Area.

agenda

The programme of work of a UN organ or conference. Each one of them must adopt its agenda as one of its first acts. Usually this is based on a provisional agenda prepared in advance and circulated as a **pre-session document** by the **conference secretariat** in consultation with the parties and the **presiding officer**. The agenda is provisional until adopted in accordance with the **rules of procedure** or other relevant authority.

Agenda 21

A set of principles and actions for development on an environmentally sustainable basis, adopted at **UNCED**, at Rio de Janeiro, in 1992.

Agenda for Peace

A 1992 report by the **Secretary-General** on ways of strengthening UN capacity for preventive diplomacy, peacemaking and peacekeeping which was followed by the Supplement to an Agenda for Peace in 1995.

www.un.org/Docs/SG/agpeace.html

agreement

Often used interchangeably with the word "treaty". For its specific legal meaning, see UN Treaty Collection - Treaty Reference Guide.

untreaty.un.org/

11

AITIC

Agency for International Trade Information and Cooperation. An intergovernmental organization based in Geneva that assists less-advantaged countries.

www.acici.org/aitic/

ALADI

Spanish abbreviation for the Latin American Integration Association established by the 1980 Montevideo Treaty by twelve Member Countries. **Mercosur** (involving only part of the membership) is sometimes described as one of the achievements of ALADI's objectives.

www.aladi.org

Amber box

(WTO) A type of agricultural subsidy that Member States have agreed to reduce. See **Blue box** and **Green box**.

ambit claim

(Negotiation) A demand or proposal which represents a **delegation**'s maximum ambition but considerably exceeds what it expects to achieve.

amendment

1. An alteration or addition to an existing legal instrument, e.g. an amendment to a convention, treaty or protocol.
2. A modification to a proposal (draft resolution, decision or other text) under debate or negotiation, formally proposed by someone other than the **sponsor**(s) of the proposal. See **revision**.

Antarctic Treaty

Provides for peaceful scientific cooperation in Antarctica and demilitarizes the continent zone. Entered into force in 1961.

AOSIS

Alliance of Small Island States. A caucus group of 43 small island and low-lying coastal States in the climate change negotiations. Has also functioned at a number of other conferences in the UN system.

www.sidsnet.org/aosis

APEC

Asia-Pacific Economic Cooperation. A forum that was established in 1989 to promote economic integration around the Pacific Rim and to sustain economic growth. APEC currently has 21 members.

www.apec.org

Arria Formula

A meeting format of the members of the **Security Council** with representatives of non-Council members and/or other entities, including NGOs, in an informal and confidential environment. Unlike the meetings or informal consultations of the **Security Council**, Arria Formula meetings are neither announced nor recorded in the **Journal of the United Nations** and since they are not meetings of the Council, its **Rules of Procedure** do not apply.

ASEAN

Association of Southeast Asian Nations. A now 10-member regional community founded in 1967 with the aim to accelerate economic growth and social progress, as well as to promote peace and security.

www.aseansec.org

ASEM

Asia – Europe Meeting. An informal process of dialogue and cooperation between the EU and 13 Asian countries with summits taking place every two years. Occasionally other States are invited to attend the summits.

www.aseminfoboard.org

ASG

Assistant **Secretary-General**.

Asian Group

The **GA electoral group** composed of States from Asia and the Pacific Island Countries (**PIC**). In most **specialized agencies**, these States are in different electoral groups. However, the Asian Group plus Turkey caucuses in a number of conferences.

assessed contribution

The contribution (expressed as a percentage of the budget of an organization) which a Member State is obligated to pay. Assessed contributions take account of each Member State's GDP.

ASSET

(IAEA) Assessment of Safety Significant Event Team.

ATCM

Antarctic Treaty Consultative Meeting. The annual conference of the Parties to the Treaty.

ATS

Antarctic Treaty Secretariat.

www.ats.org.ar

Australia Group

An informal arrangement which aims to allow exporting or transhipping countries to minimize the risk of assisting chemical and biological weapon proliferation.

www.australiagroup.net

B

backloading

(Trade and other agreements) Ensuring that the impact of commitments is mainly felt towards the end of a phase-in period. See **frontloading**.

Bangkok, Treaty of

Shorthand for the South East Asia **Nuclear Weapon Free Zone** Treaty. Adopted in 1995.

Basel Convention

Shorthand for the Convention on the Control of Transboundary Movements of Hazardous Wastes and their Disposal. A global agreement for addressing the problems and challenges posed by hazardous waste, which entered into force in 1989. Its **Secretariat** is administered by **UNEP** and regular **COP**s are held.

www.basel.int

Basel Protocol

Shorthand for the 1999 Basel Protocol on Liability and Compensation establishing rules on liability and compensation for damages caused by accidental spills of hazardous waste during export, import or during disposal.

Beijing

Informal shorthand for the Fourth World Conference on Women (**FWCW**) held in Beijing in 1995 and the Declaration and Platform for Action adopted on that occasion. See **CSW**.

Berlin Mandate

(UNFCCC) Adopted at **COP**1 of the **UNFCCC** and led to the **Kyoto Protocol**.

Bern Convention

Refers to at least two international instruments:
1. Shorthand for the Bern Convention of 1886 for the Protection of Literary and Artistic Works, one of the two cornerstones of the **WIPO** Treaty System. See **Paris Convention**;
2. Shorthand for the Convention on the Conservation of European Wildlife and Natural Habitats, adopted in 1974.

Bern Union

(WIPO) The International Union for the Protection of Literary and Artistic Works. See **Paris Union**.

Bicycle Theory

(Informal) A suggestion that if a process does not continue to make progress at an adequate rate, it will 'fall over'.

BIE

International Bureau of Exhibitions (from the initials of *Bureau International des Expositions* in French). An international organization dealing with the frequency and quality of world exhibitions. Not to be confused with **IBE**.

www.bie-paris.org

binding (adjective)

Which gives rise to an obligation under international law. As contrasted, for example, with a **declaratory** resolution, a voluntary code of conduct or a political commitment.

binding (noun)

(WTO) A synonym for 'concession', e.g. an enforceable legal obligation not to raise tariffs above a rate specified in a country's 'schedule of concessions'.

BIS

Bank for International Settlements (in Basel, Switzerland), whose members are central banks.

www.bis.org/

19

black box

Analogy to a box whose contents cannot be seen. Used as a noun, adjective or verb in a number of contexts. For example: 1. (Negotiation) 'One element of the package is still a black box', meaning that the specifics of that element are as yet not established; 2. (Arms control verification) 'These industrial facilities are black boxed', meaning that the agreement provides that they are exempt from inspection because adequate assurance can be obtained in other ways, such as monitoring what goes in and out of them.

Blue box

(WTO) A type of agricultural subsidy involving compensatory payments for production limitation/limiting programmes. See **Amber box** and **Green box**.

BPOA

Barbados Programme of Action to assist the sustainable development of **SIDS**. Adopted in 1994, it was followed by the Mauritius Strategy for the implementation of the Programme of Action in 2005.

www.sidsnet.org

Board of Directors

(World Bank and IFC) The **Executive Council** of these organizations.

Board of Governors

1. (IAEA) The **Executive Committee** of the Agency.
2. (World Bank) The **General Conference** of the **IBRD**, **IDA** and **IFC**.

bogged down

(Negotiation) A less formal equivalent of '**stalled**' but with greater implied optimism that progress could resume. It is mainly used in sentences such as 'let us not get bogged down on details, but look instead at the broader picture'. See **breakdown** and **stalemate**.

Bonn Convention

See **CMS**.

Bonn Guidelines

(CBD) Shorthand for the Bonn Guidelines on Access to Genetic Resources and Fair and Equitable Sharing of the Benefits Arising out of their Utilization. Adopted by **COP** 6 in 2002.

BONUCA

UN Peace-Building Office in the Central African Republic.

bracketing

The process of inserting square **brackets** around non-agreed text in documents under negotiation.

brackets (square)

Used in documents under negotiation to indicate that the bracketed words or text are not yet agreed by the conference.

Brahimi Report

Report of the Panel on UN Peace Operations chaired by Lakhdar Brahimi. See **DPKO**.

www.un.org/Depts/dpko/lessons

break (noun)

(Negotiation) An agreed temporary interruption, to allow participants to rest, collect their thoughts, consult, etc.

breakdown

(Negotiation) A point at which negotiations make no progress and the participants see no prospect of agreement. See **stalemate**, **bogged down** and **stalled**.

break off

(Negotiation) To withdraw from negotiations, to put an end to them. Can be temporary or final.

breakthrough

(Negotiation) The removal of a major obstacle to agreement, suggesting that the negotiations can now progress towards a satisfactory outcome.

Bretton Woods Institutions

The **IMF** and the **IBRD** created by the Bretton Woods Agreement at the UN Monetary and Financial Conference in 1944.

BRICSA

A **caucus group** composed of Brazil, Russia, India, China and South Africa, which has met at summit level.

Brundtland Commission

The World Commission on Environment and Development, convened by the UN and chaired by Norwegian Prime Minister Gro Harlem Brundtland. The Commission's Report, *Our Common Future* (1987), popularized the notion of 'sustainable development'.

BTWC

Biological and Toxin Weapons Convention. Shorthand for the Convention on the Prohibition of the Development, Production and Stockpiling of Bacteriological and Toxin Weapons and on Their Destruction. Entered into force in 1975.

www.opbw.org

bundling/unbundling

(Negotiation) A technique that refers to the aggregation or separation of **agenda** items or issues.

bureau

1. The formal leadership of the conference. The specific composition of the bureau is usually enumerated in the **rules of procedure,** but it usually consists of the president, vice-president(s), (or the chairman, vice-chairmen) and **rapporteur**. In some conferences, the bureau, sometimes assisted by the conference secretary, meets as a **steering committee**.
2. (In some organizations) The **secretariat**.

BWC or BWT

See **BTWC**.

www.opbw.org

C

CA

(UPU) The Council of Administration, the **Executive Committee** of **UPU**.

CACAM

(UNFCCC) A **caucus** group in the climate change negotiations comprising countries of Central Asia and the Caucasus, Albania and Moldova.

Cairns Group

(WTO) A broad-based **coalition** of States established in 1986 to support agricultural trade liberalization. The Cairns Group currently numbers eighteen members from four continents.

www.cairns.org

Cairo

Informal shorthand for the International Conference on Population and Development held in Cairo in 1994 or the Programme of Action it adopted.

Cancun

Informal shorthand for the **WTO** Fifth Ministerial Conference, held in Cancún, Mexico, in 2003.

CANZ

An electoral sub-group in **WEOG** and a **caucus group** in a range of conferences, composed of Canada, Australia and New Zealand.

CAP

(EU) Common Agricultural Policy.

CARICOM

Caribbean Community and Common Market. Promotes the integration of the economies of its Member States and the coordination of their foreign policies. The Community acts as a **caucus group** in some international conferences.

Cartagena Protocol

(CBD) Agreement on Biosafety adopted by the **CBD COP** in 2000.

www.biodiv.org/biosafety/

carve-out

(Negotiation) An agreement to exempt a portion of the subject matter (e.g. a specified economic activity) from the application of an agreement.

CASA

(DDA) **Coordination Action on Small Arms**.

cast a vote (verb)

To vote.

CAT

Committee Against Torture. Composed of ten experts appointed by the State Parties of the Convention Against Torture and Other Cruel, Inhuman or Degrading Treatment or Punishment (1984). The State Parties must report every four years to the Committee.

caucus (verb)

To meet as a caucus, prior to or during conferences.

caucus group

A group of **delegations** which meet in the margins of international conferences, and in some cases outside them, to discuss issues relevant to the conference(s) and in some cases seek to develop common positions.

CBD

UN Convention on Biological Diversity. Adopted at the **Rio** Earth Summit and entered into force in 1994. The Convention establishes three main goals: the conservation of biological diversity, the sustainable use of its components and the fair and equitable sharing of the benefits from the use of genetic resources. **Secretariat** in Montreal and regular **COP**s are held.

www.biodiv.org

CCAMLR

(Antarctic Treaty) Convention for the Conservation of Antarctic Marine Living Resources. The same initials are used for the Commission which is the implementing agency for the Convention.

www.ccamlr.org

CCO

(UNAIDS) Committee of Co-sponsoring Organizations.

CCP

(FAO) Committee on Commodity Problems.

CCPCJ

Commission on Crime Prevention and Criminal Justice. One of the **functional commissions** of **ECOSOC**.

CCW Convention

Convention on Prohibitions or Restrictions on the Use of Certain Conventional Weapons Which May Be Deemed to Be Excessively Injurious or to Have Indiscriminate Effects of 1981. Often referred to as the 'Inhumane Weapons' Convention.

CD

The **Conference on Disarmament**.

CDB

1. Caribbean Development Bank. One of the **regional development banks**.

www.caribank.org

2. Common Data Base of the United Nations Statistical Division.

unstats.un.org/unsd/cdb/

CDM

(UNFCCC/KP) Clean Development Mechanism. One of the three mechanisms for implementation of the **Kyoto Protocol**.

cdm.unfccc.int/

CEB

UN System's Chief Executives Board of Coordination. Replacing the former Administrative Committee on Coordination (ACC).

ceb.unsystem.org

CEDAW

Committee on the Elimination of Discrimination Against Women. Composed of 23 experts appointed in accordance with the Convention of the same name.

www.un.org/womenwatch/daw/cedaw/

CEIT

Countries with Economies in Transition.

CEN-SAD

The Community of Sahel-Saharan States. Established in 1998 as a framework for integration and complementarity.

www.cen-sad.org/

CER

Closer Economic Relationship between Australia and New Zealand. A regional economic integration arrangement which interacts with others, e.g. **AFTA**-CER.

CERD

Committee for the Elimination of Racial Discrimination. Composed of eighteen experts elected in accordance with the Convention of the same name and reporting to the **GA**.

CERN

European Organization for Nuclear Research based on the Franco-Swiss border near Geneva.

www.cern.ch

CESCR

(ECOSOC) Committee on Economic, Social and Cultural Rights, which functions as the **COP** of the International Covenant on Economic, Social and Cultural Rights.

CFCs

Chlorofluorocarbons. A category of chemical substances that destroy the ozone layer. Regulated by the **Montreal Protocol**.

CFS

(FAO) Committee on World Food Security.

chair

The **presiding officer** of a conference.

chairman

Title of a **presiding officer** (often of a **committee**, **working group**, **expert group** or **caucus group**). The term chairman is gender-neutral and is correct, although 'chair' and 'chairperson' are also used in practice. The title '**president**' tends to be reserved for the **plenary sessions** of major conferences.

chairman's text, draft or compilation text

A draft text introduced by the presiding officer in an attempt to help the conference towards agreement. It can include some words or text in square **brackets**, indicating that the issues to which they relate are for later resolution. A chairman's draft is often an attempt at a final text that might secure consensus. A chairman's compilation, on the contrary, only puts together a number of competing proposals submitted by **delegates**.

Chinese Taipei

(WTO and APEC) The formal name of Taiwan.

CHOGM

Commonwealth Heads of Government Meeting.

CHR

Commission on Human Rights. Not to be confused with **HRC**.

www.ohchr.org

CICP

(UNODC) Centre for International Crime Prevention.

CIGEPS

(UNESCO) Intergovernmental Committee for Physical Education and Sport, a sub-organ of the UNESCO **General Conference**.

CIS

Commonwealth of Independent States.

CITES

Convention on International Trade in Endangered Species of Wild Fauna and Flora. Entered into force 1975. Regular **COP**s. **Secretariat** in Geneva.

www.cites.org

CLIPS

(WMO) Climate Information and Prediction Services.

Closed door (briefing/meeting)

One to which access is restricted to the members of the relevant conference, committee or organization.

CMS

Convention for the Conservation of Migratory Species of Wild Animals (or **Bonn Convention**). Entered into force in 1983. Regular **COP**s. Serviced by the **UNEP**/CMS **Secretariat** in Bonn.

www.cms.int

CND

Commission on Narcotic Drugs.

COAG

(FAO) Committee on Agriculture.

coalition

A group of States or **delegations** which work together for a particular objective.

Codex Alimentarius

Publication on food standards maintained by a joint **FAO/WHO** Commission.

www.codexalimentarius.net/

COFI

(FAO) Committee on Fisheries.

COFO

(FAO) Committee on Forests.

COMESA

Common Market for Eastern and Southern Africa. Created in 1994 and covering 22 States in that region.

Commission on Narcotic Drugs

A **functional commission** of **ECOSOC**. The main policy-making body for the United Nations on drug-related matters. It is also the governing body of **UNDCP**.

www.unodc.org

Commission on Population and Development

A **functional commission** of **ECOSOC**, mandated to monitor and assess the implementation of the Programme of Action adopted by **ICPD**.

Commission on Science and Technology for Development

A **functional commission** of ECOSOC.

committee

A subsidiary conference, often composed of a subset of the members of a larger conference (e.g. **executive committee)**, but in some cases open to all delegations (e.g. **main committees** and a **committee of the whole**). Any organ or conference may create one or more committees to perform a particular task (e.g. **drafting committee)**, to address a particular issue (e.g. **credentials committee**) or a particular set of **agenda** items (e.g. **main committees**). In some cases, some of these committees are institutionalized by the statute of an international organization or other such formal authority. Committees can debate and at times negotiate and make recommendations to their parent body; they cannot make decisions on behalf of that body.

committee of the whole (COW)

Sometimes established by a conference to facilitate discussion and negotiation. Like other committees, the power of the COW is limited to making recommendations for adoption by the conference in **plenary** meeting.

Committee on Conferences

(GA) A permanent subsidiary of the **GA** which makes recommendations on the calendar of conferences.

Committee on Information

(GA)   Dealing with the United Nations public information policies and activities.

www.un.org/ga/coi/

Commonwealth

A community of States, most of which were part of the former British Empire. The Commonwealth does not normally **caucus** in UN meetings but does hold conferences of its own.

www.thecommonwealth.org

Commonwealth of Independent States

A community of States and economic union composed of twelve of the former constituent republics of the Soviet Union. See **CIS**.

www.cisstat.com

communication

1. Any formal message transmitted from one entity to another, as, for example, from a **secretariat** to the Member States. See **notification**.
2. (CHR) A complaint to **CHR** from an individual or group alleging violations of human rights (the Commission has established procedures for considering such communications).

compensatory finance (schemes)

Intergovernmental arrangements to reduce the impact of fluctuations in commodity prices for national economies which are especially vulnerable to them. The **IMF** Compensatory and Contingency Financing Facility and the **EU**'s STABEX (for **ACP** countries) are two examples.

concession

1. (Negotiation) Something which is agreed by one party with a view to meeting the concerns of another.
2. (WTO) A legally enforceable commitment to reduce a tariff or to remove a restriction on the trade in services.

conference of the parties (COP)

A number of treaties, including several of the environmental and human rights conventions, provide for meetings of the COP to oversee the implementation of the convention or **protocol** and to approve its budget and financial regulations. The COP can also provide guidance, receive reports and make recommendations to the parties. COPs convene usually on an annual or biannual basis. Some are serviced by permanent **secretariats**. See **MOP**.

Conference on Disarmament

The single multilateral negotiating forum for arms control and disarmament, established by **UNSSOD**1, but not technically a UN body in that it determines its own membership and is not subsidiary to any UN body.

disarmament2.un.org/cd/

37

CONGO

(ECOSOC) Committee on NGOs. Assesses NGOs seeking **consultative status**.

consensus

A procedure whereby a conference takes a decision without a vote. Consensus is distinct from unanimity in that it can coexist with differing views, to a degree. The **presiding officer** determines whether consensus exists (or 'has been reached') in the light of the views expressed by delegations and his/her assessment of 'the sense of the meeting'. Like all decisions by presiding officers, such determinations are subject to their acceptance by the conference. Most UN bodies have refrained from limiting their presiding officer's freedom of action by defining the term in their **rules of procedure**. Despite or because of its subtle and flexible meaning, consensus is the preferred mode of decision-making in all conferences and the only one in many.

constituency

1. A body of opinion and/or interests to which a government, representative or leader must be responsive.
2. A body of opinion and/or interest which is capable of being represented (e.g. "At this conference, there would be a constituency for someone who argued that (...) ")
3. (GEF) The Member Countries that a GEF Council Member represents.

consult (verb)

To talk to another **delegation**, the **secretariat**, or home authorities, with a view to learning their views.

consultation

1. The action of consulting.
2. (WTO) The first stage of the WTO dispute settlement procedure which requires the parties to a dispute to hold discussions (possibly involving a mediator) with a view to resolving the dispute.

consultations of the whole

(Security Council) Informal consultations which may only include Members of the **Security Council** and **Secretariat**.

Consultative Party

(Antarctic Treaty) A Party to the Treaty which is entitled to participate in decision-making in the **ATCM.** Consultative status is linked to the scale of scientific research undertaken in Antarctica. The other Parties to the Treaty are called 'non-Consultative Parties'.

consultative status

1. A formal relationship with **ECOSOC** which may be granted to not-for-profit public **NGO**s under certain conditions. Consultative status tends to help achieve **observer** status at UN conferences.
2. (Antarctic Treaty) The status of Consultative Parties.

contact group

A condensed forum for discussion and/or negotiation, with the objective of assisting the process of forging **consensus**. Contact groups are often convened by **presiding officers**. They count as **informal consultations** and have no formal, decision-making status. See **informal contact group**.

Contestability of a market, (international)

(WTO) The extent to which, from the view point of an exporter, a market is free from distortions due to regulation or other action by the government or to monopolies, cartels, etc.

contracting party (State)

The **Vienna Convention** on the Law of Treaties defines 'contracting State' as 'a State which has consented to be bound by the treaty, whether or not the treaty has entered into force.'

Convention on Wetlands

See the **Ramsar Convention**.

convoy problem

(Negotiation) A reference to the fact that a group can only progress at the rate of the slowest of its members. See **lowest common denominator**.

COP or CoP

Conference of the parties to a convention or other treaty. See **MOP**.

COP1, COP2, COP3, etc.

First, second, third, etc. **session** or **meeting** of the Conference of the Parties (to a particular treaty).

Copenhagen Consensus

An attempt by a group of independent economists in 2004 to prioritize projects for improving global welfare.

www.copenhagenconsensus.com

Copenhagen Declaration

Adopted by world leaders at the World Summit for Social Development in 1995.

COP/MOP

(Some environmental conventions) Conference of the Parties to the Convention serving also as a Meeting of the Parties to a **protocol**.

COPUOS or UNCOPUOS

United Nations Committee on the Peaceful Uses of Outer Space. A subsidiary body of the **GA**. Meets in Vienna.

corridors

Traditionally conference corridors and lobbies, but includes anywhere other than in the formal work of the conference, where delegations engage in the informal exchanges, negotiations, **caucus** meetings, etc. By extension, those exchanges, caucus meetings, etc. themselves. 'Corridor work' is engaging in such activities.

co-sponsor

A **delegation** which joins others in proposing a **resolution** or other formal proposal for adoption by a conference.

Cotonou Agreement

A trade agreement signed between the **EU** and 77 **ACP** countries in 2000. Replaces the **Lomé Conventions**. This agreement provides that the non-reciprocal trade preferences from the EU are to be removed after a transition period (2002-2007) during which negotiations of **EPAs** will take place.

council

Name of the **executive committee** of several of the **specialized agencies**.

Countries with economies in transition

Countries with formerly centrally planned economies and undergoing transition to market oriented ones. See **CEIT**.

COW

Committee of the whole.

CPF

Collaborative Partnership on Forests. Involves fourteen international organizations and supports **UNFF**.

CRC

Committee on the Rights of the Child. Composed of ten experts elected in accordance with the Convention of the same name.

http://www.unicef.org/crc/crc.htm

credentials

A document signed by the Head of State or Government (or in some cases another high authority) to establish the status of:

1. a representative to the United Nations, its Offices and other international organizations; or

2. a **delegate** or delegation to an international conference. Without credentials in good order, a person is not a delegate and cannot legally vote or otherwise act on behalf of his/her State (or other sending entity). See **full powers**.

credentials committee

A committee **mandated** to review the credentials of **delegations**, ensure that they are properly accredited by an authority which is entitled to be represented at that conference, and report to the **plenary** of a conference.

CRP

1. Conference room paper. A text distributed by the conference **secretariat** as an aid to debate as opposed to a formal proposal. See **working paper**.

2. (IAEA) Coordinated Research Project.

CSD

Commission on Sustainable Development. A **Functional Commission** of ECOSOC. Established to monitor the implementation of **Agenda 21**.

CSOCD

Commission for Social Development. A **Functional Commission** of ECOSOC. Established to monitor the implementation of the 1995 Social Summit in **Copenhagen**.

CSW

Commission on the Status of Women. A **Functional Commission** of ECOSOC mandated, inter alia, to monitor implementation of the Platform for Action of the Fourth World Conference on Women (**FWCW**).

CTBT

Comprehensive Nuclear-Test-Ban Treaty, adopted in 1996. Prohibits all nuclear test explosions.

www.ctbto.org

CTBTO Preparatory Commission

(CTBT) The Preparatory Commission for the implementation of the CTBT and the first **COP**.

www.ctbto.org

45

CWC

Convention on the Prohibition of the Development, Production, Stockpiling and Use of Chemical Weapons and on Their Destruction. Entered into force in 1997. Often abbreviated as Chemical Weapons Convention. See **OPCW**.

www.opcw.org

D

DAC

(OECD) Development Assistance Committee.

www.oecd.org/dac

DAW

(UN Secretariat) Division for the Advancement of Women.

www.un.org/womenwatch/daw/

DDA

(UN Secretariat) Department for Disarmament Affairs.

disarmament2.un.org/

DDG

Deputy **Director-General**.

de minimis

(WTO) 'Too small to warrant regulation'. Examples include 'de minimis imports', 'de minimis subsidies' and 'de minimis dumping margins', each of which define the lower limits below which otherwise applicable regulations do not apply or responses are not permissible *(Latin,* abbreviation for *de minimis non curat lex* meaning 'the law is not concerned about trivial matters').

Decalogue

(CD) The ten subject areas on which the **Conference on Disarmament** has decided to work.

declaration

A formal statement of special significance issued by ministers (Ministerial Declaration) or **delegates** at the closure of a conference, summit or other event. Declarations may be legally binding but usually are not. See UN Treaty Collection - Treaty Reference Guide .

untreaty.un.org/

declaratory

Which declares an intention or opinion etc., as opposed to expressing an agreed commitment.

declaratory interpretation

A statement made at the time of signature or **ratification** in which a State spells out its interpretation of one or more of the provisions of the treaty. Here the term 'declaratory' emphasizes the contrast with 'agreed'.

delegate

A representative of a State or organization who has been authorized to speak and act on its behalf and who has been duly accredited to a conference.

delegation

A team of **delegates**.

delegation station

An office of the conference **secretariat** from which conference documents are distributed and where duplicates may be requested.

deliberative forum

A conference that can discuss issues and make recommendations but cannot negotiate treaty texts.

DESA

(UN Secretariat) Department of Economic and Social Affairs.

www.un.org/esa/desa.htm

DG

Director-General.

Digital Agenda

(WIPO) The work programme for the Organization responding to the confluence of the Internet, digital technologies and the intellectual property system.

www.wipo.int

Digital Solidarity Fund

Established at the first segment of the **WSIS** in 2003, the fund supports development projects aimed at reducing information society disparities between and within countries.

www.dsf-fsn.org

diplomatic conference

A conference of **plenipotentiaries**, held for the purpose of initialling or signing a multilateral treaty. The text of the agreement has usually been settled before the diplomatic conference convenes.

diplomatic hour

A reference to the practice of 'stopping the clock' to prolong a **meeting** or a negotiation beyond its previously agreed finishing time. (A mistranslation of the French for 'diplomatic time').

Director-General

The title of the chief executives of several of the **specialized agencies**.

disqualified from voting

Not entitled to vote, e.g. because **credentials** are not in order or because of non-payment of assessed contribution. See **not financial/non-financial**.

DM

(UN Secretariat) Department of Management.

DMAB

(UPU) Direct Mail Advisory Board.

DNA

(UNFCCC/KP) Designated National Authority. The national agency representing a government taking part in **CDM/JI** projects under the **Kyoto Protocol**.

Doha

(WTO) Informal shorthand for the **WTO** Fourth Ministerial Conference, held in Doha, Qatar, in 2001.

Doha Development Round

(WTO) The current round of multilateral trade negotiations which were launched in **Doha**.

DPA

(UN Secretariat) Department of Political Affairs.

DPI

(UN Secretariat) Department of Public Information.

DPKO

(UN Secretariat) Department of Peacekeeping Operations.
www.un.org/Depts/dpko/dpko/

drafting group (or informal drafting group)

An informal group created by the **presiding officer** or the conference/**committee** that meets in private to expedite the process of drafting an agreed text. A text produced by a drafting group has no status until adopted by the **parent body**.

DSB

(WTO) Dispute Settlement Body.

www.wto.org

DSF

Digital Solidarity Fund.

DSG

Deputy **Secretary-General**. The second highest rank in the UN **Secretariat**.

Dublin Group

A group of like-minded donor countries which meet to exchange information and sometimes coordinate their actions in relation to anti-drug assistance programmes to developing countries.

E

E10

Elected ten Members of the **Security Council**. See **P5**.

early harvest

(Negotiation) Benefits for the parties to an **agreement** which are received soon after its conclusion, as contrasted with those that may take a number of years to eventuate. 'Proposing an early harvest' can mean inviting other parties to an agreement or impending agreement to take steps to ensure that it yields benefits for the parties earlier than previously envisaged.

Eastern European Group

An **electoral group** in the **GA** and many other international organizations, composed of the former communist countries of Europe and the former Soviet Union. Occasionally functions as a **caucus**, but most of its members also participate in **Western Group** meetings as observers.

EBRD

European Bank for Reconstruction and Development. The **regional development bank** for Europe.

www.ebrd.com

EC

European Community.

ECA

(ECOSOC) Economic Commission for Africa (in Addis Ababa). One of the **regional commissions** of ECOSOC.

www.uneca.org

ECE

(ECOSOC) Economic Commission for Europe (in Geneva). One of the **regional commissions** of ECOSOC.

www.unece.org

ECLAC

(ECOSOC) Economic Commission for Latin America and the Caribbean (in Santiago). One of the **regional commissions** of ECOSOC.

www.eclac.org

eco-

An abbreviation for 'ecological', used as a prefix to create a new term relating to protection of the natural environment (e.g. eco-labeling, eco-accounting, etc.).

ECOSOC

United Nations Economic and Social Council. One of the **principal organs** of the UN.

www.un.org/docs/ecosoc/

ECOWAS

Economic Community of West African States. Established in 1976 to promote economic integration and political co-operation.

EFTA

European Free Trade Association. A free trade area among Iceland, Liechtenstein, Norway and Switzerland.

www.efta.int/

Electoral groups

The groups into which **delegations** are divided for electoral purposes and for other purposes where **geographical equity** or **representation** is wanted (e.g. the distribution of **bureau** positions in a large conference). The **GA** and each of the **specialized agencies** have different electoral groups. In general, electoral groups do not **caucus** on political issues, although a small number of **regional groups** (notably the **African Group** and **GRULAC**) are both electoral and caucus groups.

electronic voting

A way of voting in which **delegates** register their vote by pressing a button (as contrasted with a **show of hands** or **roll-call**).

Emergency Special Session

(GA) A **session** called at very short notice in accordance with resolution 377 A (V) (Uniting for Peace) when a deadlock occurs in the **Security Council**.

Employer delegate

(ILO) A member of a Member State **delegation** to the **International Labour Conference** who represents the employers of that State. Each delegation to this Conference consists of two delegates appointed by the government and two others nominated in agreement with the most representative national organizations of employers and workers respectively. See **worker delegate**.

endorsed candidate

A candidate supported by an **electoral group**.

Environmental Integrity Group

(UNFCCC) A **caucus group** in the climate change negotiations, consisting of Mexico, the Republic of Korea and Switzerland, in addition to several other Parties, to uphold 'environment integrity' while recognizing the need for **flexibility**.

Environmental Management Group (EMG)

Created in 1999 by the **GA** with the aim to enhance cooperation in the fields of environment and human settlements within and beyond the UN system. Chaired by the **Executive Director** of **UNEP**. **Secretariat** based in Geneva.

www.unemg.org

EPA

(EU / ACP) Economic Partnership Agreements. By 2008, EPAs will replace the **Lomé Accords** and the **Cotonou Agreement** governing trade relations between the ACP countries and the EU.

ESCAP

(ECOSOC) United Nations Economic and Social Commission for Asia and the Pacific (in Bangkok). One of the **regional commissions** of ECOSOC.

www.unescap.org

ESCWA

(ECOSOC) Economic and Social Commission for Western Asia (in Beirut). One of the **regional commissions** of ECOSOC.

www.escwa.org.lb

EU

European Union.

European Community (EC)

The precursor of the European Union and the collective term for the European Coal and Steel Community, the European Economic Community and the European Atomic Energy Community. Note that EC is not an accepted abbreviation for the **European Commission**.

European Union (EU)

The European regional integration organization in which the Member States partly pool their sovereignty. It is a member in its own right of several international organizations and a party to various treaties, in some cases alongside its Member States. The European Commission (one of the principal institutions of the EU) has competence in a number of fields, notably trade, and as such participates in the work of several international conferences, notably in the WTO. In other conferences the Member States routinely caucus and seek to develop common positions, sometimes in association with other States, especially those which aspire to join the Union.

www.europa.eu.int

ex officio

By virtue of his/her position or function *(Latin)*.

Executive Committee, Board or Council

A body elected from the membership of an international organization to provide direction and oversight to the work of the organization or one of its programmes, in between meetings of the **General Conference**. In some organizations it has a different title (e.g. in the IAEA 'Board of Governors', in ILO 'Governing Body' and in **ICAO**, **ITU** and **IMO** among others it is known as 'Council').

Executive Director

1. The title of the chief executives of several of the **specialized agencies** and UN programmes.
2. (ILO) The second highest rank in the **Secretariat**.
3. (World Bank) A member of the Board of Directors.

expert group

A subsidiary conference formed to discuss issues at a technical (as opposed to political) level and sometimes to make recommendations to the **parent conference**. The members of such groups are often appointed or elected in their personal capacities.

expert meeting

Informal meeting of representatives of governments, intergovernmental and non-governmental organizations, scientific bodies and academia to discuss scientific, technical or other issues. Participation in such meetings is by invitation.

extended bureau

Composed of both the present and previous **bureau** members of a conference. It operates at some conferences with the purpose of ensuring the smooth transition from one **session** to another.

extraterritoriality

An attempt by a State to apply its laws beyond its jurisdiction or conversely to juridically excise part of the territory of a State so that its laws no longer apply there. Although widely condemned in theory, the principle has some benign applications, e.g. the extraterritoriality or immunity enjoyed by diplomatic missions, and laws which punish nationals who engage in pedophilia or corruption in other jurisdictions.

F

FAO

Food and Agriculture Organization of the United Nations (in Rome). One of the **specialized agencies**.

www.fao.org

FCCC

See **UNFCCC**.

FCTC

(WHO) Framework Convention on Tobacco Control. Entered into force in 2005.

www.who.int/tobacco/framework/

Fifth Committee

(GA) One of the **Main Committees**. Deals with administrative and budgetary issues.

final act

A solemn document sometimes adopted by a major conference at the end of its work, which may include a report on the conference but whose main point is an important decision or declaration.

FIPS

(WTO) Five interested parties. A **contact group** to address questions of agricultural trade composed of Australia, Brazil, India, the **EU** and the USA.

First Committee

(GA) One of the **Main Committees**. Deals with disarmament and international security.

flexibility

1. (Negotiation) Willingness to adjust one's position and take (some) account of the concerns of others.
2. (UNFCCC/KP) A characteristic given to the three mechanisms of implementation under the **Kyoto Protocol**.

floor

1. The part of the conference room where the **delegates** have their assigned seats, e.g. 'speaking from the floor' as opposed to 'from the **rostrum**'.
2. By extension, the delegates, e.g. 'the speaker tried to persuade the floor'.
3. By extension of 2, 'to take the floor' is to start speaking to the **meeting** or to make an **intervention**.
4. By extension of 3, permission (from the **presiding officer**) to speak to the meeting. 'To seek the floor' is to ask the **presiding officer** for his/her permission to address the meeting, as in 'the delegate sought the floor and the **chair** gave it to him.' 'Microphone' is an informal synonym for meaning 4.

FMCT

Fissile Material Cut-off Treaty. Long called for by the **GA** and currently under negotiation among a limited number of countries. It would ban the production of weapons grade nuclear material.

FoC or FOC

Friend of the chair.

focal point

An official or agency designated by a government to serve as the focus or channel of communications on a particular topic. Some organizations may have two types of focal points, such as the **GEF** which has political and operational focal points.

formal informals

The most formal of the informal **meetings** in the **committees** of the **General Assembly** or some other intergovernmental forums. Formal informals are off-the-record meetings with no sound recordings or press releases.

Fourth Committee

(GA) One of the **Main Committees**. Alternative name for the **Special Political and Decolonization Committee**.

Francophonie

Informal shorthand for the *Organisation Internationale de la Francophonie* (OIF). The intergovernmental organization of French-speaking States and Governments at the political level. The OIF is active but does not normally **caucus** in UN conferences. The *Agence Intergouvernementale de la Francophonie* (AIF) is the OIF's agency for technical cooperation.

www.francophonie.org

freedom

Many different rights conferred by multilateral agreements.
1. (ICAO) e.g. First, Second, etc. Freedom. The right to carry certain categories of passengers or freight on a specified route.
2. (WTO) e.g. Freedom of Transit. The right to transport goods unhindered across the territory of another party.
3. (Law of the Sea) Circumscribed rights of unhindered transit or navigation.

friend of the chair

A **delegate** who has been **mandated** by the **presiding officer** to undertake a task, usually that of finding **consensus** on a particular issue or body of issues.

friends of the chair

A group of friends of the chair. A **contact group** convened by the **presiding officer**.

friends of the rapporteur

A **contact group** convened by the **rapporteur**, or members of such a group. This term derives from '**friends of the chair**' and is only used in some conferences.

frontloading

(Trade and other agreements) Ensuring that the impact of commitments is mainly felt towards the beginning of a phase-in period. See **backloading**.

full powers

A document authorizing a representative to sign a legal instrument on behalf of a State. Heads of State, Heads of Government and Ministers of Foreign Affairs do not need to present full powers, since they are considered as representatives of a State for all acts related to negotiating and adopting international legal instruments. See **credentials**.

functional commissions

(ECOSOC) **Subsidiary bodies** established to assist **ECOSOC** in the performance of its functions.

FWCW

Fourth World Conference on Women held in Beijing in 1995 which adopted a Declaration and Platform for Action. See **Beijing** and **CSW**.

G

G4

Coalition of Brazil, Germany, India and Japan on the proposed expansion of the **Security Council**.

G5

(Trade negotiations) A **caucus group** composed of Canada, Costa Rica, Chile, Mexico and the USA.

G6

(Trade negotiations) The G5 plus Panama.

G7

The seven largest Western economies. **Summits** of the Heads of State/Government have now evolved to the **G8**, but there are still **meetings** of the G7 ministers of finance, among others.

G8

Annual **meeting** of Heads of State/Government or ministers of the seven largest Western economies and Russia together with the Commission of the **European Union**. Originally dealing exclusively with international financial issues, it now also addresses other pressing global problems.

G9

(Informal) The G8 (drawing attention to the fact that, with the EU, it actually has nine members).

G10

1. (International financial institutions) A **caucus group** of finance ministers and central bank governors of major **OECD** Member Countries. It also meets at the level of deputies and has a number of **working groups**.
2. (Nuclear non-proliferation) A **ginger group** which seeks to forge **consensus** in support of nuclear non-proliferation.

G11

Also known as the Cartagena Group. A forum of debtor countries in Latin America.

G20

1. (Trade negotiations) A **caucus group** of developing countries formed at the **Cancun** Conference. It has a particular focus on trade in agricultural products.
2. (Economic policies) An informal forum for the finance ministries and central banks of major industrial nations and emerging-market countries to discuss and seek agreement on the international monetary and financial system and other international economic questions.

G24

The Intergovernmental Group of Twenty-Four on International Monetary Affairs and Development. A **caucus group** of developing countries established in 1971. China participates as 'Special Invitee'.

G33

(Trade negotiations) A **caucus group** of developing countries formed just before the **Cancun** Conference, focusing on proposals for 'special products' and a 'special safeguard mechanism'.

G77

Established in 1964 at the first session of the United Nations Conference on Trade and Development (**UNCTAD**). It seeks to harmonize the positions of developing countries, articulate their collective economic interests and promote its negotiating capacity. Although China is not officially a member of the group, it almost always supports the group's position. Statements made on behalf of the G77 are given precedence in the **speakers list** over statements made by the **African Group, GRULAC** and other groups whose members are also members of the G77.

www.g77.org

G90

(Trade negotiations) A **caucus group** of the **ACP** and **African Union** countries and **LDC**s formed at the **Cancun** Conference.

GA

United Nations **General Assembly**. See **UNGA**.

www.un.org/ga

GATS

(WTO) General Agreement on Trade and Services of 1995.

GATT

The 1947 General Agreement on Trade and Tariffs, the precursor of **WTO**.

gavel (noun or verb)

A wooden hammer used by a **presiding officer**. By extension, a symbolic metaphor for his/her office (e.g. 'to hand the gavel over to a vice-president' meaning the task of presiding over the meeting). Other meanings (especially of the verb) relate to the uses a **presiding officer** makes of the gavel to communicate with the **floor**. For example: 'to gavel down objections' meaning to silence **delegations** which are vociferously raising objections, by recalling them **to order**, by repeatedly striking the gavel, or 'to gavel through a decision', meaning to strike the gavel once, signifying that a decision has been taken, without allowing enough time for any delegation to raise an objection.

GCOS

(WMO) Global Climate Observing System.

GDLN

Global Development Learning Network. Initiated by the **World Bank** in 2004 as a global partnership of learning centres using **ICT** to connect people working in development.

www.gdln.org

GEF

Global Environment Facility.

www.gefweb.org

General Assembly

One of the **principal organs** of the UN. All the Member States are represented in the **GA** and have one vote. Regular **sessions** are held from September to December. **Special** or **emergency special sessions** may also take place. See **main committee** and **subsidiary body**.

www.un.org/ga

General Committee

(GA) Committee composed of the President and the twenty-one vice-presidents of the **GA** and the chairmen of the six **Main Committees**.

general conference

A conference of the entire membership of an international organization which discusses the work of the organization and takes administrative decisions. Several of the **specialized agencies** use the term 'assembly' or 'congress'.

General Council

The standing decision-making body of the **WTO**, composed of representatives of all Member States. It also meets, under different rules, as the Dispute Settlement Body (**DSB**) and the Trade Policy Review Body.

general debate

An early stage of the **GA** and other major conferences in which **delegation** leaders make formal statements, often prepared in capitals.

general document

A document circulated by a conference **secretariat** which is neither **limited** nor **restricted**.

Geneva Conventions

A number of **conventions** have been adopted in Geneva but the term usually refers to four Conventions adopted in 1949 (and to which 190 States are now **Parties**) on International Humanitarian Law. They provide legal safeguard that cover the way wars may be fought and the protection of individuals.

www.icrc.org

Geneva Group

A caucus group of major contributors to the budgets of various international organizations and programmes which discusses and at times develops common positions on budgetary issues.

geographical balance, equity or representation

The distribution of seats between **electoral groups** in accordance with a formula in the **rules of procedure** or other authority.

geographical groups

An alternative term for **regional groups** (although many of these are not based on geography). It refers ambiguously either to **electoral groups** or **caucus groups**.

GHG

Greenhouse Gas. A gas responsible for climate change.

GHS

(Environment) Globally Harmonized System of Classification and Labelling of Chemicals, managed by an **ECOSOC subcommittee** of experts.

ginger group

(Informal) A **like-minded group** of **delegations** dedicated to promoting a particular idea or philosophy.

Global Compact

An initiative launched by Secretary-General Kofi Annan in 1999 that would bring companies on board with UN agencies, civil society and labour to support now ten principles in the areas of human rights, labour, anti-corruption and the environment.

www.unglobalcompact.org

Global Environment Facility (GEF)

An inter-agency instrument created in 1991 to help developing countries fund projects and programmes that protect the global environment. Although **GEF** is an independent organization, its implementing agencies are **UNEP**, **UNDP** and the **IBRD**.

www.gefweb.org

Global Fund

Shorthand for the Global Fund to Fight AIDS, Malaria and Tuberculosis. A non-UN financial instrument created as a partnership among governments, civil society, the private sector and affected communities to finance the fight against the three diseases.

www.theglobalfund.org

GMEF

(UNEP) Global Ministerial Environment Forum. An open forum on environmental policy which is held during the yearly session of the UNEP **Governing Council**.

Governing Body

1. (ILO) The **Executive Committee** of the ILO.
2. (IAEA) The **Board of Governors** and the **General Conference** are referred to as 'the governing bodies of IAEA'.
3. (UNAIDS) The Programme Coordinating Body (**PCB**).

GPA

(UNEP) Global Programme of Action for the protection of the marine environment from land-based activities.

www.gpa.unep.org

grandfather clause

A provision in an agreement which exempts the consequences of actions taken before the agreement enters into force. Hence the verb 'to grandfather' something, meaning to apply such an exemption to it.

Green box

(WTO) A category of domestic support measures for agricultural producers exempted from restriction because they have minimal impact on trade. An example is disaster relief. See **Amber box** and **Blue box**.

Green Room

(WTO) An informal negotiating forum initiated by the Director-General of **GATT** during the **Uruguay Round** negotiations to discuss and draft compromise texts on specific items among a small group of invited countries. The Green Room process continues in the context of WTO, and sometimes takes the form of 'mini-ministerial' meetings prior to or during WTO Ministerial Conferences.

GRID

(UNEP) Global Resources Information Database, which underpins UNEP's Environmental Assessment Programme.
www.grid.unep.ch/

Group of Latin American and Caribbean Countries (GRULAC)

An **electoral group** at the **GA** and in most **specialized agencies** which also functions as a **like-minded caucus group** at many conferences.

group spokesman/spokesperson

A delegate who speaks on behalf of a group.

group statement

A statement made on behalf of a group of **delegations** (usually **like-minded**) which have decided to make a joint statement. These are normally given precedence in the **speakers' list** over statements made in the name of a single delegation.

GRULAC

Group of Latin American and Caribbean Countries.

GUUAM

A political, economic and strategic alliance uniting Georgia, Ukraine, Uzbekistan, Azerbaijan and Moldova. **Caucuses** in the United Nations.

www.guuam.org/

H

Habitat

UN-HABITAT.

Hague Rules

A number of conventions have been signed at The Hague. Refers here to the shorthand for the International Convention for the Unification of Certain Rules of Law relating to Bills of Lading, adopted in 1924. Establishes liability rules for carriers for loss or damage of goods carried at sea.

HDI

Human Development Index. A summary composite index prepared by **UNDP** and measuring a country's average achievements in three elements of human development: a long and healthy life, knowledge and a decent standard of living.

www.hdr.undp.org

HFCs

Hydrofluorocarbons. A category of chemical substances covered by the **UNFCCC/KP**. Not to be confused with **CFC**s.

HIPC

Heavily Indebted Poor Countries.

HIPC Initiative

A framework launched in 1996 by the **World Bank** and **IMF** with the objective of reducing the external debt of 27 **HIPC**s.

HLCM

High Level Committee on Management. The principal inter-agency body of the UN system for coordination on administrative and management issues.

ceb.unsystem.org/hlcm/

HLCP

High Level Committee on Programmes. The principal inter-agency body of the UN system for coordination of programmes across the UN system.

ceb.unsystem.org/hlcp/

HONLEA

(CND) Regional meetings of Heads of National Drug Law Enforcement Agencies. A subsidiary body of **CND**.

host (country) Government

1. The Government of the country in which an international organization is located or in which an international conference takes place.
2. The Government of a country organizing a conference.

79

host country agreement

The agreement between a **host country Government** and an international organization providing **immunities and privileges** and other administrative arrangements for the organization and delegations attending its **meetings**.

HRC

UN Human Rights Committee. Composed of eighteen experts elected in accordance with the International Covenant on Civil and Political Rights. Not to be confused with **CHR**.

www.ohchr.org

humanitarian coordinator (HC)

(DPKO) In the context of peacekeeping operations, responsible for planning and coordination of humanitarian operations.

I

IADB

Inter-American Development Bank. The **regional development bank** for Latin America and the Caribbean.

www.iadb.org

IAEA

International Atomic Energy Agency (in Vienna). Not a **specialized agency**, but it reports annually to the **GA** and occasionally to the **SC**.

www.iaea.org

IBE and ICE

1. International Bureau of Education. The name of a pre-existing international organization that merged with **UNESCO**, now applied to an international centre for comparative education in Geneva which is an autonomous body that is also an integral part of UNESCO. It organizes regular International Conferences on Education (ICE).

www.ibe.unesco.org

2. Anglicized form of **BIE.**

IBRD

International Bank for Reconstruction and Development. One of the **specialized agencies**. Its members are members of the **IMF** which have accepted the IBRD Articles.

www.worldbank.org

ICAO

International Civil Aviation Organization. One of the **specialized agencies** with headquarters in Montreal.

www.icao.int

ICC

International Criminal Court (in The Hague). Any individual who has committed a crime falling under the provisions of the **Rome Statute**, which entered into force in 2002, is liable for prosecution by the Court. Not to be confused with **ICJ**.

www.icc-cpi.int

ICGFI

International Consultative Group on Food Irradiation. An expert group established at the initiative of **WHO**, **FAO** and **IAEA**. Its **Secretariat** is the Joint FAO-IAEA Division on Nuclear Techniques in Food and Agriculture.

ICJ

International Court of Justice (in The Hague). One of the principal organs of the UN. Not to be confused with **ICC**.

www.icj-cij.org

ICPD

International Conference on Population and Development. Adopted a Programme of Action in Cairo (1994).

ICPRCP

(UNESCO) Intergovernmental Committee for Promoting the Return of Cultural Property to its Countries of Origin or its Restitution in Case of Illicit Appropriation, a sub-organ of the UNESCO **General Conference**.

ICRC

International Committee of the Red Cross. An independent neutral organization with a permanent mandate in international humanitarian law under the **Geneva Conventions**.

www.icrc.org

ICRCRC

International Conference of the Red Cross and the Red Crescent on international humanitarian law and humanitarian action. Held every five years and attended by **delegations** from States and national Red Cross or Red Crescent Societies, the **IFRC** and the **ICRC**. A standing commission operates between conferences.

ICSC

International Civil Service Commission. Coordinates the conditions of service of staff in the UN common system.

www.icsc.un.org

ICSID

International Centre for the Settlement of Investment Disputes. An independent organization closely linked to the **World Bank** and established under the Convention on the Settlement of Investment Disputes between States and Nationals of Other States of 1966.

www.worldbank.org/icsid

ICT

Information and communication technologies.

ICTP

Abdus Salam International Centre for Theoretical Physics.

IDA

(World Bank) International Development Association. It provides interest-free loans and grants to the poorest developing countries.

www.worldbank.org/ida

IDB

1. Islamic Development Bank. A **regional development bank** to foster the economic development and social progress of member countries and Muslim communities in accordance with the principles of Shari'ah (Islamic Law).

www.isdb.org

2. An alternative abbreviation for **IADB**, the Inter-American Development Bank.

www.iadb.org

IEA

International Energy Agency. Created by **OECD** Member Countries committing themselves to take effective measures to meet any oil supply emergency and, over the long term, to reduce dependence on oil.

www.iea.org

IFAD

International Fund for Agricultural Development. One of the **specialized agencies** with headquarters in Rome.

www.ifad.org

IFAP

(UNESCO) Intergovernmental Council for the Information for All Programme, a sub-organ of the UNESCO **General Conference**.

www.unesco.org/webworld/ifap

85

IFC

International Financial Corporation. Promotes sustainable private sector investment in developing countries. Although a separate **specialized agency**, it is closely affiliated with the **World Bank**, sharing the same President and the same individuals as Governors and Directors (except in so far as some **IBRD** members are not members of IFC), but the IFC has its own staff.

www.ifc.org

IFCC

(G77) The Intergovernmental Follow-up and Coordination Committee on Economic Cooperation among Developing Countries. Meets every two years at the senior officials' level to review the implementation of the Caracas Programme of Action adopted by the **G77** in 1981.

IFIs

International financial institutions.

IFRC

International Federation of the Red Cross and Red Crescent Societies.

www.ifrc.org

IGAD

Intergovernmental Authority for Development. The East African Economic Community which was formed in 1986.

ww.igad.dj

IGCP

(UNESCO) International Geological Correlations Programme, a sub-organ of the UNESCO **General Conference**.

IHP

(UNESCO) Intergovernmental Council for the International Hydrological Programme, a sub-organ of the **UNESCO General Conference**.

ILC

1. **International Law Commission**.
2. The same initials are sometimes used for the **International Labour Conference**.

ILO

International Labour Organization. One of the **specialized agencies** with headquarters in Geneva.

www.ilo.org

IMO

International Maritime Organization. One of the **specialized agencies** with headquarters in London.

www.imo.org

IMPACT Project

(WIPO) A project to fully automate the operation of the **PCT**.

Impasse

(Negotiation) A point beyond which progress is not possible.

In extenso

In full; how a statement is to be recorded in the **summary records** or **conference report** *(Latin)*.

INC

Intergovernmental negotiating committee.

INCB

International Narcotics Control Board.

INFCIRC

(IAEA) Information circular.

informal consultations

1. Exchanges of views among **delegations** which may extend to attempts at mutual persuasion or to informal negotiation and which take place outside the formal conference debate. 2. A meeting convened for the purpose of an informal exchange of views. At such a meeting the **rules of procedure** of the conference do not apply; there is normally no record and no **interpretation**.

Informal Consultations Other Than Those of the Whole

(Security Council) Refers to consultations, such as the 'group of friends' and the '**contact group**', usually formed around a specific issue. The group of friends is the venue where an issue is introduced to those interested. The contact group usually takes an active role in the implementation of Council decisions on that issue.

informal contact group

Established for representatives of different **caucuses** or **delegates** to meet privately to discuss specific **agenda** items or issues, bridge differences and achieve **consensus**. In some negotiating forums, observers may be invited to attend such groups.

informal informals

(UN New York) Informal consultations so-called to distinguish them from those formally convened and notified in the **Journal of the United Nations**.

inhumane weapons

See **CCW Convention**.

INSTRAW

UN International Research and Training Institute for the Advancement of Women, (in Santo Domingo) guided by a Board of Trustees appointed by **ECOSOC**.

www.un-instraw.org

instrument of ratification

A document signed by a head of State or minister of foreign affairs, which legally binds a State to a treaty and its obligations once the treaty has entered into force.

intergovernmental agreement

So-called to differentiate it from a 'treaty' or 'international agreement' which is only between or among States.

intergovernmental negotiating committee

An ad hoc forum for the purpose of negotiating an international legal instrument, such as a framework convention.

International Bureau

(UPU) **Secretariat** of the Union.

international civil servant

A member of the staff of the UN or another international organization who has an international legal status.

international financial institutions

Sometimes used to mean the **IMF** and **the World Bank Group**, but sometimes extended to include the **regional development banks**, the **GEF** and even the **BIS**.

International Labour Conference

The annual conference of the Member States of ILO.

International Labour Office

The **Secretariat** of the **ILO**.

International Law Commission

Composed of 34 members elected by the **GA**. It promotes the progressive development of international law and its codification.

www.un.org/law/ilc

International Narcotics Control Board

A quasi judicial control organ for the implementation of the United Nations drug conventions. Its thirteen members are elected by **ECOSOC** and serve in their personal capacities.

www.incb.org

INTERPOL

International Criminal Police Organization based in Lyon.

www.interpol.int

interpretation

A simultaneous oral translation of a statement made at a meeting. This term is also used in its everyday and legal meanings.

intervene, intervention

When a **delegate**, having been given permission to speak by the **presiding officer**, makes a statement, he or she 'intervenes' in the debate. His or her statement is an 'intervention'.

IOC

(UNESCO) Intergovernmental Oceanographic Commission, a sub-organ of UNESCO **General Conference**.

IOM

International Organization for Migration.

www.iom.int

IOR-ARC

Indian Ocean Rim Association for Regional Cooperation.

IPCC

(WMO/UNEP) Intergovernmental Panel on Climate Change. Established by WMO and UNEP to assess scientific, technical, socio-economic impacts on climate change.

www.ipcc.ch

IPDC

(UNESCO) Intergovernmental Council of the International Programme for the Development Communications, a sub-organ of **UNESCO General Conference**.

IPRs

Intellectual property rights.

ISA

International Seabed Authority (in Kingston). An autonomous international organization established under **UNCLOS**.

www.isa.org.jm

ISO

International Organization for Standardization (in Geneva). An international **non-governmental organization**.

www.iso.org

IT

Information technology.

ITC

International Trade Centre (based in Geneva). The technical cooperation agency of **WTO** and **UNCTAD** for operational and enterprise-oriented aspects of international trade and development.

www.intracen.org

ITLOS

International Tribunal for the Law of the Sea (in Hamburg).

www.itlos.org

ITTA

International Tropical Timber Agreement. Successive commodity agreements negotiated under **UNCTAD**, the last of which entered into force in 1997. See **ITTO**.

ITTO

International Tropical Timber Organization (in Yokohama). Services the **ITTA**.

www.itto.or.jp

ITU

International Telecommunication Union. One of the **specialized agencies** with headquarters in Geneva.

www.itu.int

IUCN

The World Conservation Union (in Gland, Switzerland). Formerly the International Union for the Conservation of Nature and Natural Resources. An organization composed of States, government agencies and **NGO**s.

www.iucn.org

IWC

International Whaling Commission. The implementing agency for the International Convention for the Regulation of Whaling.

www.iwcoffice.org

J

Joint Inspection Unit

Established by and reporting to the **GA** but whose mandate covers the whole UN system. Based in Geneva.

JI

(UNFCCC/KP) Joint Implementation. One of the three mechanisms for implementation of the **Kyoto Protocol**.

JIU

Joint Inspection Unit.

Journal of the United Nations

(UN New York) A calendar of UN meetings, agendas and events (including unofficial meetings) in New York and issued daily in English and French.

www.un.org/Docs/journal/en/lateste.pdf

JUSCANZ/JUSSCANNZ

A **caucus group** that makes joint statements in the climate change (and other environmental) negotiations. The composition of this group has evolved and now includes Japan, US, Switzerland, Canada, Australia, Norway and New Zealand. Depending on the issues and the forum, a number of other **delegations** may participate, including Iceland, Mexico, the Republic of Korea, Russia and others.

K

killer amendment

(Informal) An amendment that changes the meaning of the original text in such a way that if it is adopted, the original text would become meaningless.

KP

Kyoto Protocol.

Kyoto Protocol

(UNFCCC) Provides for binding emission reductions for Annex I Parties to the **UNFCCC**. Entered into force in 2005.

www.unfccc.int

L

L document

See **limited document**.

language

(Negotiation) A set of words, a formulation. As in 'I propose alternative language for this paragraph'.

LDCs

Least Developed Countries.

LDC Fund

(UNFCCC) Established by the **COP** to assist **LDC**s to undertake programmes of action to adapt to climate change.

LDC Group

A **G77** subgroup now numbering 50 least developed States and which caucuses widely in UN and other forums.

LDC Expert Group (LEG)

(UNFCCC) A panel of twelve experts providing advice to **LDCs** on the preparation and implementation of National Adaptation Programmes of Action (**NAPAs**).

lead sponsor

One of the co-**sponsors** that takes responsibility for tabling a **resolution**.

Least Developed Countries

The countries lowest on the scale of development according to low income, human resource weakness and economic vulnerability criteria.

www.un.org/ohrlls/

least formals or informal, informals informals

The most informal of meetings. These meetings take place between two or more **delegates** in various contexts outside of a **session**. As contrasted with **informal consultations** which have a residual element of formality in that they are convened.

like-minded group

Group of **delegations** which share a common view on a body of issues considered at an international conference. They often make **group statements** or work together to develop proposals to be advanced in the name of their group. As like-mindedness is issue specific, there are different like-minded groups in different conferences.

Like-Minded Megadiverse Countries

(CBD) A **caucus group** of megadiverse developing countries that collectively account for 70 per cent of the world's biodiversity. The group formed in 2002 with the aim to leverage negotiating strength in the field of access to genetic resources and benefit-sharing (**ABS**).

limited document

Document of a temporary nature, notably draft **resolutions** or decisions. Documents in this category are identified with the letter **L**.

LLDC

1. Landlocked Developing Countries. A **caucus group** which meets annually at the ministerial level.
2. (WTO & UNCTAD) Previously these initials were used for **least developed countries**, but these organizations now use the same abbreviation as other UN bodies (i.e. **LDC**s).

LMMC

Like-Minded Megadiverse Countries.

LMG

Like-minded group.

LMO

(Cartagena Protocol) Living modified organism.

Lomé Convention

Agreement between the **EU** and the **ACP** countries, adopted in 1975 and subsequently renegotiated four times (Lomé II, III, IV and the **Cotonou Agreement** in 2000). Under this agreement, ACP countries benefit from non-reciprocal trade preferences with the EU. This regime will be replaced by **EPA**s by 2008.

London Convention

(IMO) Shorthand for the Convention on the Prevention of Marine Pollution by Dumping Waste and Other Matter. Entered into force in 1972.

www.londonconvention.org

low hanging fruit

(Negotiation) 'Picking the low hanging fruit' means securing agreement on matters which can readily be agreed before attempting negotiation on more difficult matters.

lowest common denominator

(Negotiation) Smallest issue/set of issues on which a conference, **meeting**, etc. can agree. See **convoy problem**.

LRTAP

(ECE) Shorthand for the 1979 Convention on Long-range Transboundary Air Pollution. Extended by eight Protocols.

http://www.unece.org/env/lrtap/

LTP

(WMO) Long-term Plan.

LULUCF

(UNFCCC) Land-use, land-use change and forestry.

M

MAB

(UNESCO) International Coordinating Council of the Programme on Man and the Biosphere, a sub-organ of the UNESCO **General Conference**.

main committee

(In large conferences only) A committee established to address part of the **agenda** of the conference (the other parts being allocated to one or more other main committees). The term distinguishes main committees from those with more restricted mandates. There are six Main Committees in the **GA**.

major donors

A **caucus group** composed of at least some of the larger contributors to the budget of an organization or programme.

major groups

(UNDESA) A category of non-governmental actors identified during the **prep-com sessions** of the 1992 **UNCED**. There are nine groups: women, children and youth, indigenous peoples, **NGO**s, local authorities, workers and trade unions, business and industry, scientific and technical community and farmers.

www.un.org/esa/sustdev/mgroupsMain.htm

mandate

1. (Noun) What a conference, organization or individual has been given authority or purpose to do. 'Remit' is a synonym.
2. (Verb) To give authority or purpose to a conference, an organization or an individual.
3. (Adjective: mandated) Who or which has been given authority or purpose.

MARPOL

Shorthand for the International Convention for the Prevention of Pollution from Ships of 1973. Modified by the 1978 Protocol.

Marrakesh Accords

1. (WTO) The agreements bringing to a conclusion the **Uruguay Round** and establishing the WTO.
2. (UNFCCC) A series of decisions adopted at **COP**7 in relation to the **Kyoto Protocol**, including emissions trading, **CDM**, and the establishment of capacity development funds.

MAT

(Cartagena Protocol) Mutually agreed terms.

MDGs

Millennium Development Goals. Eight quantified targets for making substantial progress by 2015 towards the elimination of poverty, to which the 191 Member States committed themselves at the **Millennium Summit**.

www.un.org/millenniumgoals/

MEA

1. Multilateral environmental agreement. A generic term for multilateral treaties relating to the environment.
2. Millennium Ecosystem Assessment. A global work programme launched by **Secretary-General** Kofi Annan in 2001 and completed in 2005.

www.millenniumassessment.org

meeting

1. The conference (as in 'the meeting decided…').
2. The conference as one in a series of conferences (as in 'the 2004 meeting of the World Health Assembly').
3. A particular day or half day of the conference, (as in 'this morning's meeting'). '**Session**' is a synonym for 2 and 3; '**sitting**' is a synonym for 3.

Meeting of members of the Security Council

Not a meeting of the **Security Council**, but an informal meeting of the members to consult with dignitaries from Member States and possibly other representatives from outside the Council.

Megadiverse Countries

(IUCN) Seventeen developed and developing countries identified by the World Conservation Monitoring Centre (**WCMC**) in 2000 which account for 70 per cent of the world's biodiversity. Not identical to the membership of **LMMC**.

105

Member State/Country

A State which is a member of an organization, usually as a result of its being a party to the treaty establishing the organization. Some organizations use the term Member Country.

memorandum of understanding

An informal type of international instrument which does not require ratification. Used more frequently in bilateral agreements. See United Nations Treaty Collection - Treaty Reference Guide.

untreaty.un.org/

MERCOSUR

Contraction of the Spanish for 'Common Market of the South'. The customs union created by Argentina, Brazil, Paraguay and Uruguay in 1991.

www.mercosur.org

MFA

Multifibre Arrangement. The predecessor to **WTO**'s Agreement on Textiles and Clothing.

MFN

(International trade) Most-favoured-nation. A fundamental principle requiring a party not to discriminate between or among trading partners.

Miami Group

(Cartagena Protocol) A **caucus group** comprising essentially Argentina, Australia, Canada, Chile, the United States and Uruguay, which are large, grain-exporting countries and have invested considerably in genetic engineering.

microcredit

A small amount of money loaned to a client by a bank or other institution.

microfinance

Funding for very small-scale commercial enterprises.

microphone

(Informal) Permission (from the **presiding officer**) to speak, as in 'several **delegates** were asking for the microphone'. The reference is to the microphone at each delegation's desk which is only switched on when the presiding officer has given that delegate permission to address the conference.

MIF

(IADB) Multilateral Investment Fund. A fund to assist private sector development in Latin America and the Caribbean with a special emphasis on micro-enterprise and small business.

MIGA

Multilateral Investments Guarantee Agency. An independent organization closely linked to the **World Bank** which acts as insurer to private investors and adviser to countries on foreign investment, with a view to assisting development in the developing countries.

www.miga.org

Millennium Development Declaration and Millenium Summit

At the Millenium **Summit** in 2000, 191 governments committed themselves, through the Millenium Development Declaration, to an **agenda** for the elimination of global poverty, notably through the implementation of the Millenium Development Goals (**MDG**s).

un.org/millenniumgoals/

Mine Ban Treaty

See **Ottawa Convention**.

MINUCI

(DPKO) UN Mission in Côte d'Ivoire.

www.un.org/Depts/dpko/missions/minuci/

MINURSO

(DPKO) UN Mission for the Referendum in Southern Sahara.

www.un.org/Depts/dpko/missions/minurso/

MINUSTAH

(DPKO) UN Stabilization Mission in Haïti.

www.un.org/Depts/dpko/missions/minustah/

Montreal Protocol

Shorthand for the Montreal Protocol (to the 1985 **Vienna Convention** for the Protection of the Ozone Layer) on Substances That Deplete the Ozone Layer. Provides for a phase-out of ozone depleting substances (**ODS**). Holds annual **COP**s. Serviced by the **Ozone Secretariat**.

MONUC

(DPKO) UN Mission in the Democratic Republic of the Congo.

www.monuc.org/

Monterey Conference

Shorthand for the International Conference on Financing for Development, held in Monterey, Mexico, in 2002.

www.un.org/esa/ffd/ffdconf/

Monterey Consensus

The outcome of the **Monterey Conference**.

MOP

Meeting of the parties. Equivalent to **conference of the parties (COP)**, the difference is only a matter of the precise wording of particular treaties. In the major environmental instruments, for example, COP tends to be used for the convention itself and MOP for the **protocols** to those conventions. See **COP/MOP**.

MOST

1. (UNESCO) Intergovernmental Council of the International Programme for the Social Sciences, a **sub-organ** of the UNESCO **General Conference**.
2. In some countries, an abbreviation for the Ministry of Science and Technology.

motion

A formal proposal made orally on a matter of procedure, e.g. a motion to suspend the **meeting**.

move (verb)

(Debate) To formally propose that the conference take a particular action. (Used only of procedural **motions**).

MPPI

(Basel Convention) Mobile Phone Partnership Initiative.

Multilateral Fund

(Montreal Protocol) Shorthand for the Multilateral Fund for the Implementation of the **Montreal Protocol**. Provides funds to assist developing countries to implement the Montreal Protocol.

www.multilateralfund.org

mutatis mutandis

Upon changing what is required, e.g. 'the **rules of procedure** shall apply *mutatis mutandis* to the **protocol** (...)'. *(Latin)*.

MYFF

(UNDP) Multi-Year Funding Framework.

MYPOW

(CBD and UNFF) Multi-Year Programme of Work.

N

NAFTA

North American Free Trade Agreement.

www.nafta-sec-alena.org

NAM

Non-Aligned Movement.

NAPAs

(UNFCCC) National Adaptation Programmes of Action. Prepared by **LDC** Parties on urgent activities to cope with climate change.

national focal points

See **focal points.**

NATO

North Atlantic Treaty Organization. Alliance of North American and European countries to safeguard their security.

www.nato.int

NCSA

National Capacity Self-Assessment for Global Environmental Management. Launched by the **GEF** in 2001, NCSAs aim to provide countries with priority capacity needs on crosscutting global environment issues.

Negative Security Guarantees/Negative Security Assurances

(Nuclear non-proliferation and disarmament) Assurances given by nuclear-armed States that they will not use or threaten to use these weapons against States which do not posses nuclear weapons. The assurances can be unilateral or contained in treaties, notably **protocols** to **NWFZ** treaties.

NEPAD

New Partnership for African Development. An integrated socio-economic development framework for Africa adopted by the Organization of African Unity (now **African Union**) Summit in 2001.

www.nepad.org

New Agenda Coalition

(Nuclear non-proliferation and disarmament) A group of 'middle power' **delegations** which aim to promote nuclear disarmament. Members are Brazil, Egypt, Ireland, Mexico, New Zealand, South Africa and Sweden.

113

New Zealand Handbook

The United Nations Handbook published each year by the New Zealand Ministry of Foreign Affairs and Trade which provides information on the aims, structure and membership of the many bodies of the United Nations.

NFAPs

(WIPO) Nationally Focused Action Plans (for assistance to developing countries).

NGLS

Non-governmental Liaison Service. A service that promotes dialogue and cooperation on development issues between **NGO**s and the UN.

www.un-ngls.org

NGO

Non-governmental organization.

NGO Liaison Office

Established in New York, Geneva (**UNOG**), Vienna (**UNOV**) and Nairobi (**UNON**) to serve as a **focal point** for all matters pertaining to relations between the United Nations and NGOs, particularly with respect to the consultative relationship with **ECOSOC**. Among other activities, the office maintains a database and publishes a list of NGOs in **consultative status** with ECOSOC.

NMHS

(WMO) National Meteorological and Hydrological Service (of the Member States).

NNWS

(NPT) All States Parties to the **NPT** other than those which possessed nuclear weapons in 1968.

no action motion

A procedural motion permitted by the **rules of procedure** of some conferences that the conference take no action (i.e. no decision) on a draft resolution or other proposal before it. If adopted, this has the same effect as defeating the draft resolution or proposal.

Non-Aligned Movement

A group formed in 1955 of countries that were not allied to either the United States or the Soviet Union during the Cold War. Has continued as a **caucus group** of 115 developing countries on issues related to international security with the aim of developing common positions. China is not formally a member of the NAM but attends its meetings and usually supports its positions.

Non-Consultative Party

(Antarctic Treaty) A party to the Treaty which is not entitled to participate in decision-making in the **ATCM**. **Consultative status** is linked to the scale of scientific research undertaken in Antarctica.

115

non-governmental organization (NGO)

Often applied exclusively to community groups and not-for-profit organizations but strictly speaking (and in the UN system) also includes businesses and business associations. The **rules of procedure** or other decisions of most conferences specify the status NGOs may be granted. They can be full members of some organizations and their conferences, alongside **Member States** (e.g. **IUCN** and the **ICICRC**); more frequently they are restricted to the status of **observers** and in some cases have restrictions placed on their access and participation. **ECOSOC** has a formal system for granting a **consultative status** to NGOs which meet certain criteria. A number of NGOs work closely with **specialized agencies** and other UN bodies, notably as implementing agencies.

non-paper

A text distributed on an informal basis and designed to facilitate the process of negotiating an agreement. The word emphasizes the informal nature of the text: it is not a proposal (although it may foreshadow one) and does not engage its author. See **working paper**.

non-party

A State that is not a **party** to a treaty but attends **meetings** or conferences of that instrument as an observer. Sometimes referred to as a non-party observer.

non-recorded vote

A vote in which the official **records** or **conference report** record the outcome of the vote in numerical terms but not the way each **delegation** voted.

Nordic Group

An electoral sub-group within **WEOG**. Its members also **caucus** and make joint statements in some conferences.

not financial/non-financial

Colloquial expression meaning that the sending government of a **delegation** is in arrears for paying its contributions due to an organization or conference, e.g. at the UN, the **GA** may decide that such a Member State shall have no right to vote.

note verbale

The standard format for formal communications through diplomatic channels, including between missions and international organizations.

notification

A formal communication of a legal character between a State and an intergovernmental organization or **secretariat** of a convention. See United Nations Treaty Collection - Treaty Reference Guide.

www.untreaty.un.org/

117

NPT

Nuclear Non-Proliferation Treaty. Entered into force in 1970.

NSG

(Nuclear non-proliferation) **Nuclear Suppliers' Group**.

NSGs

(Nuclear non-proliferation and disarmament) **Negative Security Guarantees**.

Nuclear Suppliers' Group

(Nuclear non-proliferation) A group of Governments seeking to assist nuclear non-proliferation by applying guidelines to exports of nuclear material and/or potentially relevant equipment.

www.nuclearsuppliersgroup.org

Nuclear Weapon Free Zone

(Nuclear non-proliferation and disarmament) An area within which the possession and deployment of nuclear weapons are prohibited, and various other nuclear activities regulated by multilateral treaty. To date six **NWFZ**s have been established, covering approximately 60 per cent of the planet.

number 2 ambassador

(Informal) A deputy head of mission who happens to carry the rank of ambassador.

NWFZ

Nuclear Weapon Free Zone.

NWS

(NPT) Nuclear Weapon States, i.e. the five States which had nuclear weapons in 1968.

objection

1. A statement, either written or oral, by a State or **delegation** informing the organization, conference or **meeting** that it objects to a proposed action or commitment.
2. (IWC and some other conferences) A formal process whereby a Member State may dissociate itself from a decision of the IWC/conference and not be bound by that decision.

observer or observer delegation

A **delegation** that has only limited rights to participate in a conference. It may represent a State or other entity that is not a **party** to the relevant treaty. Observer delegations are often further sub-divided into categories such as Member States, non-member States, international organizations and **NGO**s, and seated accordingly. In all cases observers may not participate in decision-making and are not bound by any decisions taken by the conference. In some cases, the **rules of procedure** define observers and the extent of their right to participate in conferences. In some conferences this is minimal; in others it is extensive. For example, in the **CHR**, State observer delegations may co-**sponsor** resolutions.

OCHA

(UN Secretariat) Office for the Coordination of Humanitarian Affairs.

ochaonline.un.org

ODCCP

United Nations Office for Drug Control and Crime Prevention (in Vienna).

www.unodc.org

ODS

1. **Official Document System**.
2. (Montreal Protocol) Ozone depleting substance.

OECD

Organization for Economic Cooperation and Development. An organization of 30 Member Countries, with headquarters in Paris. The members of OECD **caucus** as a group in some conferences.

www.oecd.org

Official Document System (ODS)

Electronic repository for official documents published by the UN. Includes the official records version of resolutions of the **GA**, **SC**, **ECOSOC** and **Trusteeship Council**.

OHCHR

Office of the UN High Commissioner for Human Rights (in Geneva).

www.ohchr.org

OHR

Office of the High Representative and **EU** Special Representative in Bosnia and Herzegovina.

www.ohr.int

OHRLLS

(UN Secretariat) Office of the High Representative for the Least Developed Countries (**LDC**), Landlocked Developing Countries (**LLDC**) and Small Island Developing States (**SIDS**).

www.un.org/org/ohrlls

OIC

Organization of the Islamic Conference. Not to be confused with **IOC**.

www.oic-oci.org

OIOS

(UN Secretariat) Office of Internal Oversight Services.

www.un.org/Depts/oios

OLA

(UN Secretariat) Office of Legal Affairs.

ONUB

(DPKO) United Nations Operation in Burundi.

www.un.org/Depts/dpko/missions/onub/

OPANAL

Agency for the Prohibition of Nuclear Weapons in Latin America and the Caribbean. The implementing agency of the **Treaty of Tlatelolco**.

www.opanal.org

OPEC

Organization of the Petroleum Exporting Countries. An organization based in Vienna, grouping eleven governments and which seeks to achieve stable oil prices.

http://www.opec.org/

OPEC Fund

A multilateral fund to cooperate with developing countries.

http://www.opecfund.org/

OPCW

Organization for the Prohibition of Chemical Weapons (in The Hague), the implementing agency for the Chemical Weapons Convention (**CWC**).

www.opcw.org

open briefing

(Security Council) A public **meeting** at which the Council receives a briefing from a Special Envoy of the **Secretary General**, the Director-General of the **IAEA** or another official.

123

open debate

(Security Council) A public **meeting** of the Council where non-members may address members on issues before them. All non-members of the Council may participate without the right to vote, under rules 37 or 39 of the Council's provisional Rules of Procedure.

open meeting

(Security Council) A **meeting** of the Council open to the public.

order, call to

A direction by the **presiding officer** that the conference or a particular **delegate** should be silent (so as to allow the conference proceedings to take place in an orderly manner). To 'recall delegates to order' means to silence them when they are **out of order**.

order, out of

Not (behaving) in accordance with the **rules of procedure.**

orientation debate

(Security Council) A **meeting** of the Council where non-members are consulted before the Council proceeds to take action.

OSART

(IAEA) Operational Safety Review Team.

OSG

(UN Secretariat) Office of the **Secretary-General**.

www.un.org/news/ossg/sg

Ottawa Convention

Shorthand for the 1997 Convention on the Prohibition of the Use, Stockpiling, Production and Transfer or Anti-Personnel Mines and on Their Destruction, also known as the **Mine Ban Treaty**. Entered into force in 1999.

Ozone Secretariat

Based in Nairobi, it services the **Vienna Convention** and the **Montreal Protocol**.

www.unep.org/ozone

P

P5

1. The Permanent Five. The five States which have permanent seats on the **Security Council**. By tradition in most conferences, the P5 are never elected as **presiding officers**, although they may occupy that position as a result of a **rotating chairmanship**.
2. A senior-level professional rank in the United Nations.

Pacific Group

A **like-minded caucus group** that makes joint statements in some conferences on a variety of issues. It consists of the Pacific Island States, Australia and New Zealand.

package

(Negotiation) Several elements which cannot be separated and which have to be accepted or rejected as a whole.

Palais des Nations

The main UN conference facility and office complex in Geneva.

parallel events

Events organized by someone other than the organizers of an international conference to run concurrently with the conference. Parallel events are often organized by **NGO**s and sometimes by a government or international organization. See **side events**.

parent conference/body

The conference which established a **committee** or **working group** and to which that committee or working group must report.

Paris Consultations

(GEF) A formalized **contact group** to discuss such issues as future replenishments of the Facility.

Paris Convention

Shorthand for the Paris Convention of 1883 for the Protection of Industrial Property, one of the two cornerstones of the **WIPO** Treaty System. See **Bern Convention**.

www.wipo.int/treaties/en/ip/paris/

Paris Union

(WIPO) The International Union for the Protection of Industrial Property. See **Bern Union**.

party

A State, international organization or regional economic integration organization which has consented to be bound by an international instrument and for which that international instrument is in force. See **contracting party**.

pass

An identity document issued at **registration** and which gives access to a particular conference. Without a pass, **delegation** members may be denied entrance to the conference venue.

PCB

1. (UNAIDS) Programme Coordinating Body, the **Governing Body** of UNAIDS, elected by **ECOSOC**.
2. (Stockholm Convention) Polychlorinated biphenyls. Listed as one of the **POP**s.

PCT

(WIPO) Patent Cooperation Treaty (1970). Provides for a single patent application valid for all States Parties.

www.wipo.int/ipdl

Pelindaba, Treaty of

Shorthand for the African **Nuclear Weapon Free Zone** Treaty, adopted in 1996.

permanent mission

A diplomatic mission accredited to an international organization.

permanent representative (PR)

The head of a **permanent mission**. For some organizations the title may be different (e.g. for the **IAEA**, the head is a **resident representative**).

PFCs

Perfluorocarbons. A category of chemicals covered in the **UNFCCC**.

PFII

Permanent Forum on Indigenous Issues.

http://www.un.org/esa/socdev/unpfii/

PIC

1. Abbreviation for Pacific Island Countries.
2. (Rotterdam Convention) Prior informed consent.

www.pic.int/

PII

(UNESCO) Intergovernmental Committee for the Intergovernmental Informatics Programme, a sub-organ of the UNESCO **General Conference**.

PKO

Peacekeeping Operation(s) of the UN. See **DPKO**.

www.un.org/Depts/dpk

Plenary

1. The whole conference meeting as such (as opposed to a **committee of the whole**) and therefore able to take decisions.
2. Full. (Plenary powers is another term for **full powers**).

Plenipotentiary

1. (noun) An individual who carries **full powers**.
2. (adjective) Said of a conference or **meeting** where the **delegation** leaders carry **full powers**.

Plenipotentiary Conference

(ITU) The **general conference** of the Union, held every four years.

PLT

(WIPO) Patent Law Treaty of 2000.

POC

1. (CD) **Point of contact**
2. (UPU) The Postal Operations Council. An elected body which makes recommendations to the Council of Administration (**CA**).

podium

A (usually raised) desk, facing the **floor**, at which the **presiding officer**, **conference secretary** and sometimes other conference officers such as the **rapporteur** sit.

point of contact

(CD) A **delegate** mandated by the chairman to lead **informal consultations** on a body of issues. The selection of **POC**s must take account of **geographical equity**.

point of order

A question as to whether the present proceedings are in order or whether a particular action by a **delegate** or a **presiding officer** follows the **rules of procedure**. Points of order request the presiding officer to exercise authority.

POPs

Persistent organic pollutants. Chemicals that remain intact in the environment for long periods and become widely distributed geographically. Regulated by the **Stockholm Convention**.

www.chem.unep.ch/pops/

PPP

Public Private Partnership. A collaborative effort between public entities and the private sector. A key element of the UN programme for sustainable development.

www.undp.org/ppp/

131

précis writers

A section of a **conference secretariat** devoted to the preparation of **summary records** or other abbreviated texts.

preliminary negotiations

Negotiations that take place before and prepare the way for formal negotiations. Preliminary negotiations go beyond modalities (e.g. beyond **preparatory negotiations)** and may address substantive issues but not to the point of reaching final agreement.

pre-negotiation

Conclusive negotiation on the substance which takes place before formal negotiation. It is usually understood that issues settled in pre-negotiation will not be re-opened when formal negotiations start. Pre-negotiated means "settled before the formal negotiations start".

Prep.COM CTBTO

Preparatory Committee for the (projected) **CTBTO**.

preparatory negotiations

Negotiations about the modalities of a future negotiation that, unlike **preliminary negotiations**, do not address the substance of the issues to be negotiated.

132

Prep-Com or Prepcom

Abbreviation for preparatory **committee** (usually preparing for the creation of an international organization).

Prep-Con or Prepcon

Abbreviation for preparatory conference (usually preparing for a subsequent conference).

pre-session documents

Documents prepared for distribution prior to the conference or **meeting**. May include **non-papers** and miscellaneous, information and **limited documents**.

president

1. Title of the **presiding officer** of a major conference.
2. (GA) Elected every year on a rotating basis among the five **electoral groups** and presides over the regular, **special** and **emergency special sessions**.

presiding officer

A **delegate** elected by the conference to control the proceedings, to maintain **order** and generally to lead the work of the conference. In so doing the presiding officer acts under the authority of the conference and with its consent. Presiding officers are formally detached from their role as representative and may not speak or vote for their delegation. All **interventions** in a conference have to be addressed to the presiding officer. See **president**.

principal organs (of the UN)

The **General Assembly**, the **Security Council**, the **ECOSOC**, the **Trusteeship Council**, the International Court of Justice (**ICJ**) and the **Secretariat**.

private (closed) meeting

(Security Council) A meeting restricted to Council members and invited observers.

private (open) meeting

(Security Council) A meeting open to non-members of the Council to attend as observers.

pro tem

For the present, implicitly, a short period of time. Abbreviated from '*pro tempore*' *(Latin)*.

protocol

1. Rules of diplomatic procedure, ceremony and etiquette observed by Heads of State/Government, diplomats, government dignitaries and intergovernmental organizations.

2. A department in a Government or an international **secretariat** that deals with relations with the missions accredited to that State or organization and with the courtesies and ceremonial afforded to visiting dignitaries.

3. An international legal agreement (e.g. treaty) appended to or otherwise closely related to another agreement. The parties to a protocol do not have to be the same as the parties to the main agreement.

provisional agenda

A draft **agenda**, not yet adopted by the conference.

PV

Procès verbal. Records by the **conference secretariat** of all statements made in a conference *(French)*.

Q

Quad

(WTO) A meeting of Canada, the European Union, Japan and the United States. In multilateral trade negotiations, the most contentious issues often require agreement among these four countries as a pre-requisite for broader consensus across a wider spectrum of WTO Members.

quid pro quo

Something in exchange for something else *(Latin)*.

quorum

The minimal number of delegations that must be present for a meeting to begin or for decisions to be taken. Quorum requirements are always stated in the **rules of procedure**.

R

R document

See **restricted document**.

Ramsar Convention

Shorthand for the Convention on Wetlands of International Importance especially as Waterfowl Habitat. Adopted at Ramsar, Iran and entered into force in 1975. **COP** every three years.

www.ramsar.org

rapporteur

1. A **delegate** elected to oversee preparation of the report of a conference.
2. An individual elected or appointed to prepare a report or a series of reports (e.g. the Special Rapporteurs appointed by the Commission on Human Rights).

Raratonga, Treaty of

Shorthand for the South Pacific **Nuclear Free Zone** Treaty, adopted in 1985.

ratification

See **instrument of ratification**.

reading

(Negotiation) The process of going through a text with a view to establishing which parts of it can be provisionally agreed and which, as yet, cannot. In a second reading the provisionally agreed portions of the text are not re-opened and negotiations focus on the sections as not yet agreed. Hopefully, at the end of the second reading somewhat more of the text will have been agreed and a third and, if needed, subsequent readings can further reduce the area of disagreement until a fully agreed text is achieved.

record writers

The staff of the conference **secretariat** responsible for preparing **summary records**.

recorded vote

A vote where the way in which each **delegation** voted is reported in the official records or conference report.

regional commissions

(ECOSOC) Subsidiary bodies. The five regional commissions are: **ECA**, **ECE**, **ECLAC**, **ESCAP** and **ESCWA**.

regional development banks

Organizations that perform a similar function to the **IBRD** but restricted to a particular region (there are eight). They are not part of the UN system but cooperate closely with **IBRD** and other UN agencies.

regional groups

Can refer to either **electoral** or **caucus groups**, although neither of these are necessarily based on geographical regions.

registration (of delegates)

Before each conference, **delegation** members must register with the conference **secretariat** and be issued a pass. To obtain a **pass**, delegates must present their passports and a document establishing their status as delegation members. For some conferences, members of **permanent missions** who are already accredited to the relevant organization do not have to register. For UN New York, see also **SG.6**.

representative

Every **delegate** is a representative of a State, international organization or NGO. Delegates usually refer to each other during formal conference debate as 'the distinguished representative of/from (...)'.

reservation

Declarations made by a State upon signature, ratification, acceptance, approval or accession to a legal instrument, indicating that it wishes to exclude or alter the legal effect of certain provisions in their application to that State. See UN Treaty Collection - Treaty Reference Guide.

untreaty.un.org/

resident coordinator (RC)

Resident coordinator of the United Nations system's operational activities for development. Responsible for planning and coordination of development operations at the country level and leader of the UN country team.

resident representative (RR)

1. The Head of the United Nations Development Programme Country Office (often also performing the role of **resident coordinator**).
2. For some organizations (e.g. IAEA), the title of the head of a **permanent mission**.

resolution

A written decision by a conference. Resolutions follow a standard format, which may vary only slightly from body to body. They consist of one sentence and a number of preambular and operative paragraphs.

restraint agreement

A (to date bilateral) agreement under which a country agrees to take measures to limit e.g. its exports to another country, in exchange for that other country not itself imposing limitations or obstacles on that trade. Sometimes called 'voluntary restraint agreements' (VRAs).

restricted document

A document issued by the conference **secretariat** which, at the time of issue, is not to be made public. Such documents are identified with the letter R.

revision or revised text

An amended version of a previously **tabled** document by the author(s) or **sponsor**(s) of that document.

right of rebuttal/reply

The **rules of procedure** of many conferences provide that a **delegation** which so requests must be given an opportunity to make a brief statement in reply to a statement made by another delegation if it believes that its own position has been misunderstood or misrepresented. Also used in practice to respond to remarks which are considered injurious.

Rio

Shorthand for the UN Conference on the Environment and Development (**UNCED**) held in Rio de Janeiro in 1992 at which the **UNFCCC** and **CBD** were opened for signature, and **Agenda 21**, the Rio Declaration on the Environment and Development and the Forest Principles were adopted.

Rio Conventions

A group term for the **UNFCCC** and the **CBD** which were adopted at **Rio**. Some include **UNCCD**.

Rio Group

1. A group of eight countries (Argentina, Brazil, Chile, Colombia, Mexico, Panama, Peru and Venezuela) established to consult over important political, economic and social issues in Latin America, and to accelerate the development of Latin American integration. Earlier known as the 'Group of 8 Countries'.

2. (UN) The Rio Group on Poverty Statistics, an expert group, which aims to harness the experience and concerns of different groups and organizations in the world working on poverty statistics.

www.ibge.gov.br/poverty/default.htm

roll-call vote

One in which the **delegations** are called to vote individually, in alphabetical order. Not to be confused with '**recorded vote**'.

rolling text

(Negotiation) A text under negotiation and which is undergoing a succession of **readings**. It contains some elements of text which are agreed and others which are still subject to disagreement (in square **brackets**).

Rome Statute

Shorthand for the Rome Statute of the International Criminal Court (**ICC**). Entered into force in 2002.

rostrum

A structure, facing the **floor** and equipped with a microphone, where a speaker may stand to address the conference.

rotating chairmanship or presidency

An automatic system under which **delegations** succeed each other in exercising the office of the **presiding officer**, at regular intervals, e.g. the presidency of the **Security Council** and of the chairmanship of **CD** rotate monthly, in alphabetical order.

Rotterdam Convention

Shorthand for the Rotterdam Convention on the Prior Informed Consent (**PIC**) Procedure for Certain Hazardous Chemicals and Pesticides in International Trade. Entered into force in 2004. **Secretariat** preformed jointly by **UNEP** and **FAO**.

www.pic.int/

Rules of procedure

A set of rules adopted by a conference to govern its workings and decision-making. Rules generally only apply to the **plenary** and **committee meetings**; **informal contact groups** and other similar meetings are generally not governed by the rules of procedure.

S

SACEP

South Asia Cooperative Environment Programme. An intergovernmental organization established in 1982.

www.sacep.org

SADC

Southern African Development Community. A regional economic integration organization of fourteen Member States, established in 1992.

SAARC

South Asian Association for Regional Cooperation, established in 1985.

www.saarc-sec.org

safeguards

1. (IAEA) A set of activities by which the IAEA attempts to verify that a State is living up to its international undertakings not to use peaceful nuclear programmes for nuclear weapons purposes.
2. (WTO) Temporary measures to assist a specified industry to adjust to heightened competition.

SAFTA

South Asian Free Trade Area. Established under the **SAARC** and due to enter into force in 2006.

SBI

(CBD/UNFCCC) Subsidiary Body for Implementation.

SBSTTA

(CBD) Subsidiary Body for Scientific, Technical and Technological Advice.

SC

Security Council.

scale of assessment

An agreed formula for determining the scale of contribution due from each Member State of an organization. Typically this is proportionate to each country's per capita GDP, with special provisions for the **least developed countries**.

SCAR

(Antarctic Treaty) Scientific Committee on Antarctic Research.
www.scar.org

scrutineer

An official of a conference or a **delegate** appointed to that role, who counts the votes or who monitors the counting of the votes cast in a **secret ballot**.

seat

1. Official position in an organ, organization, committee, etc. (as in 'a permanent seat on the **Security Council**' or 'elected to sit on the **ICJ**').
2. The place at a desk reserved for a particular **delegation** or individual. As in 'to occupy or resume one's seat', meaning to sit down at one's assigned place.

Second Committee

(GA) One of the **Main Committees**. Deals with economic and financial issues.

secret ballot/vote

A vote organized to ensure that each individual **delegation** votes remains secret. Widely used for elections.

Secretariat and conference secretariat

1. The executive and administrative staff of an international organization, organized and managed as an executive body. Every **specialized agency** and many UN programmes and bodies have their own secretariats.
2. However, whenever the context does not make clear that one of these is intended, the term 'the Secretariat' refers to the UN Secretariat, one of the six **principal organs** of the United Nations. It is led by the **Secretary-General** under the direction of the Member States acting through the **GA**.
3. A conference secretariat is a team of officials, usually (but not necessarily) **international civil servants**, organized and

managed to provide administrative and support services to an international conference. Whereas the secretariat of an agency is a permanent body, a conference secretariat exists only for the duration of its specific conference, plus any necessary preparatory and post-conference activity. The UN Secretariat provides the conference secretariat for virtually all UN conferences held in New York and for many other UN conferences held elsewhere. Likewise, the secretariats of each of the **specialized agencies**, UN Programmes and **COP**s provide the conference secretariats for conferences organized under their aegis. However, some conferences need a conference secretariat of their own to be assembled from a variety of sources.

Secretariat of the Pacific Community

The **Secretariat** (in Suva) of the **South Pacific Forum** and a number of other regional organizations and arrangements.

www.spc.org.nc

Secretary-General

The Head of the UN **Secretariat**.

Security Council

One of the **principal organs** of the UN, it has primary responsibility for the maintenance of international peace and security. The Council has fifteen members: five permanent members and ten elected by the **GA** for two-year terms.

www.un.org/Docs/sc/

147

session

A series of **meetings,** e.g. 'the sixtieth regular session of the **GA** was held in 2005'.

SG

(Informal) The **Secretary-General**.

SG.6 Form

(UN New York) A form issued by the Protocol and Liaison Service of the **Secretariat** for the **accreditation** and registration of **delegates** to **meetings**. It must be completed, authorized by a cover letter from the **permanent mission** and submitted to the Pass and Identification Office at least 48 hours prior to the start of the meeting. Each delegate needing a **pass** must bring a copy of the authorized SG.6 when **registering**.

sherpas

(Informal) The officials who meet in advance to prepare a **summit** conference.

show of hands

A way of voting in which **delegations** are invited to raise a hand (or the delegation nameplate) for 'yes', 'no' or '**abstain**'. A vote by show of hands is an **non-recorded vote**.

side events

Organized by the organizers of an international conference and taking place concurrently with the conference. Typically they may include discussion groups, seminars and informal occasions for **delegates** to exchange views and explore each others thinking, and/or presentations, exhibitions for their information. As opposed to **parallel events**, side events usually take place on the conference premises.

SIDS

Small Island Developing States. A **caucus group** in the sustainable development negotiations.

www.sidsnet.org

single negotiated text

A draft text which compiles all the proposals into a coherent whole and provides a basis for further negotiation. See **chairman's text**.

sitting

A particular day or half day of the conference. **'Meeting'** is generally used as a synonym.

Sixth Committee

(GA) One of the **Main Committes**. Deals with legal issues.

SMEs

Small and medium-sized enterprises.

SNT

Single negotiated text.

South Pacific Forum

The summit level regional organization in the South Pacific, whose members are the Pacific Island Countries, Australia and New Zealand.

www.forumsec.org.fj

SPC

1. **Secretariat of the Pacific Community**.
2. (GA, informal) The **Special Political (and Decolonization) Committee**.

speakers' list

List maintained by a **presiding officer** of **delegations** which have asked to speak, in the order in which they have made the request (subject to a few exceptions).

specialized agency

An autonomous international organization joined to the UN through a special agreement.

Special envoy/representative

Individuals appointed by the **Secretary-General** who engage in preventive diplomacy and mediation in conflict and post-conflict situations, recovery operations or global issues.

Special Political (and Decolonization) Committee

(GA) One of the **Main Committees**. Also known as the **Fourth Committee**, it deals with political issues other than international security and disarmament.

special session

A session of the **GA**, outside and additional to its regularly scheduled sessions, focused on a particular issue or body of issues. Requires at least fourteen days notice. Other conferences may also be able to hold special sessions.

SPNFZ

South Pacific Nuclear Free Zone. See **Raratonga, Treaty of**.

Sponsor

The **delegation** which proposes a resolution for adoption by a conference.

SPREP

South Pacific Regional Environment Programme.

www.sprep.org.ws

SR

Summary records.

SRSG

Special Representative of the **Secretary-General**. Appointed by the Secretary-General and responsible for overall mission coordination.

stalemate

(Negotiation) A point at which negotiations make no progress and no solution is in sight.

stalled

(Negotiation) A point at which negotiations are making no progress. The implication, however, is that this may be temporary, not a **break down** or **stalemate**.

STAP

(GEF) Science and Technology Advisory Panel.

statement of explanation or by way of explanation

The statement made by a **delegation** exercising its **right of rebuttal** (most **rules of procedure** strictly limit the duration of such statements).

status quo (ante)

The way things are (were before a certain event) *(Latin)*.

steering committee

A restricted **committee** which plans the work of a major conference. It deals exclusively with procedural matters.

Stockholm

Shorthand for the UN Conference on the Human Environment of 1972. It was the beginning of UN activity in relation to the environment and development. It adopted a declaration, including 26 principles, and an action plan.

Stockholm Convention on Persistent Organic Pollutants

Concluded in 2001, entered into force in 2004. Regular **COP**s serviced by **UNEP**. See **POP**s.

www.pops.int

straw poll

(Elections) An initial round of voting, the result of which is not recorded.

Subcommission on Illicit Drug Traffic and Related Mattes in the Near and Middle East

A subsidiary body of the **CND**.

sub-committee

A **committee** created by another (parent) committee. Often the **chairman** of a sub-committee is appointed by the parent committee, not elected by the sub-committee itself.

sub-organ

(UNESCO) One of a number of intergovernmental bodies which are subsidiary to the UNESCO **General Conference**.

subsidiary body/organ

A **committee** or **working group** or even a small organization, created by and reporting to another organization or conference.

summary records (SR) of the debate

(GA and some other major conferences) Written by the **conference secretariat** and later published as a conference document. They are not adopted by the conference. **Delegations** may suggest corrections to the SR of their own statements, but **amendments** which are clearly at variance with what was said or which would add to the length or change the balance of the SR are not accepted.

summit

Conference at which the participants are Heads of State or Government.

T

table (verb)

To lodge the text with the conference **secretariat** for distribution to all **delegations** and to make an **intervention** recommending its adoption by the conference, e.g. to table a draft resolution or to table a draft treaty.

tally

The count of positive and negative votes and **abstentions**.

TDB

(UNCTAD) Trade and Development Board, the **Executive Committee** of **UNCTAD**.

terminal dues

(UPU) Payments made to a postal administration to compensate it for an imbalance between the volume of incoming and outgoing mail.

Third Committee

(GA) One of the **Main Committees**. Deals with social, humanitarian and cultural issues.

Thirty Eighth floor

(Informal, UN New York) The floor on which the Office of the **Secretary-General** of the UN is located. By extension, his office and the senior leadership of the **Secretariat**.

TK

Traditional Knowledge. Refers to knowledge, innovations and practices of indigenous and local communities, although the definition of TK may vary among organizations and conferences.

Tlatelolco, Treaty of

Shorthand for the Treaty for the Prohibition of Nuclear Weapons in Latin America and the Caribbean. Entered into force in 1969.

TLT

(WIPO) Trademarks Law Treaty of 1994.

TRAINS

(UNCTAD) Trade Analysis and Information System. A comprehensive computer-based information system on trade control measures that uses UNCTAD's database.

transparency

1. The principle that public affairs are on a sounder basis when they are conducted openly.
2. The degree to which a process is open to scrutiny, e.g. 'the treaty provides for greater transparency in (…)'.

travaux préparatoires

Preparatory work. Covers the record of negotiations and all other documents which may be of evidentiary value in establishing the meaning of an international treaty *(French)*.

TRIMS

(WTO) Trade-Related Investment Measures.

TRIPS

(WTO) Agreement on Trade-Related Aspects of Intellectual Property Rights of 1995.

Tripartite structure

(ILO) Refers to the unique three-party structure of the **ILC** comprising representatives governments, employers and workers.

Trusteeship Council

One of the **principal organs** of the UN. It suspended its operations with the independence of the last remaining United Nations trust territory, Palau, in 1994.

TSAG

(ITU) Telecommunications Standardization Advisory Group.

Turtle Bay

The geographical place name for the site of the UN headquarters building in New York.

Type II Outcome/Type II Partnership

(WSSD) One of the two outcomes of the Johannesburg Summit on Sustainable Development (2002) and taking the form of voluntary multistakeholder partnerships which contribute to the implementation of intergovernmental commitments.

U

UDRP

(WIPO Arbitration and Mediation Centre) Uniform Domain Name Dispute Resolution Policy.

UMA

Union du Maghreb Arabe. The economic community for the Maghreb region (Algeria, Libya, Mauritania, Morroco and Tunisia) founded in 1989.

www.maghrebarabe.org/

Umbrella Group

(UNFCCC/KP) A **caucus group** in the climate change negotiations composed of Australia, Canada, Iceland, Japan, New Zealand, Norway, Russian Federation, Ukraine and the United States.

UNAIDS

United Nations Programme on HIV/AIDS. Jointly sponsored by nine UN agencies. **Secretariat** in Geneva.

www.unaids.org

UNAMA

United Nations Assistance Mission in Afghanistan

www.unama.afg.org

UNAMSIL

(DPKO) United Nations Mission in Sierra Leone.
www.un.org/Depts/dpko/missions/unamsil

unanimously or by unanimity

Said of a conference decision taken with the support of all **delegations** (established by a **show of hands** or other form of voting, or by the **presiding officer** asking: 'Are we all agreed?' and no dissent being expressed.). Contrast with **consensus,** the more common form of decision-making.

UNCC

United Nations Compensation Commission. Established by the **Security Council** to process claims and pay compensation for losses resulting from Iraq's invasion and occupation of Kuwait.

UNCCD

United Nations Convention to Combat Desertification in Countries Experiencing Serious Drought and/or Desertification, especially in Africa. Entered into force in 1996.
www.unccd.int

UNCED

United Nations Conference on Environment and Development. Held at **Rio** de Janeiro in 1992. Resulted in the adoption of **Agenda 21**, the Rio Declaration on Environment and Development, the Statement of Forest Principles, the United Nations Framework Convention on Climate Change (**UNFCCC**) and the United Nations Convention on Biological Diversity (**CBD**).

UNCITRAL

United Nations Committee on International Trade Law (in Vienna).

www.uncitral.org

UNCLOS

United Nations Conference on the Law of the Sea. UNCLOS III, from 1973 to 1982, adopted a Convention of the same name which entered into force in 1994.

www.un.org/Depts/los

UNCOPUOS

United Nations Committee on the Peaceful Uses of Outer Space (in Vienna). A subsidiary body of the **GA**.

www.oosa.unvienna.org/COPUOS/copuos.html

UNCTAD

United Nations Conference on Trade and Development. A subsidiary body under the **GA**, promoting the integration of developing countries into the world economy. **Secretariat** in Geneva.

162

www.unctad.org

UNDCP

United Nations International Drug Control Programme, part of **ODCCP**.

www.unodc.org

UNDESA

United Nations Department of Economic and Social Affairs.

www.un.org/esa/desa.htm

UNDG

United Nations Development Group. An instrument for UN reform created by the **Secretary-General** in 1997 to bring together operational agencies in the UN System working on development and **MDGs**.

www.undg.org

UNDOF

(DPKO) United Nations Disengagement Observer Force on the Golan Heights.

www.un.org/Depts/dpko/missions/undof

UNDP

United Nations Development Programme (in New York). The main body responsible for coordinating UN development work.

www.undp.org

UNEP

United Nations Environment Programme (in Nairobi).

www.unep.org

UNESCO

United Nations Educational, Scientific and Cultural Organization (in Paris).

www.unesco.org

UNFCCC

United Nations Framework Convention on Climate Change. Entered into force in 1994. Regular **COP**s and serviced by a **Secretariat** in Bonn.

www.unfccc.int

UNFF

United Nations Forum on Forests.

www.un.org/esa/forests/

UNFICYP

(DPKO) United Nations Force in Cyprus.

www.unficyp.org

UNFPA

United Nations Population Fund (in New York).

www.unfpa.org

UNGA

United Nations **General Assembly**. See **GA**.

www.un.org/ga

UN-HABITAT

United Nations Human Settlements Programme (in Nairobi).

www.unhabitat.org

UNHCR

Office of the UN High Commissioner for Refugees. The UN Refugee Agency based in Geneva.

www.unhcr.ch

UNICEF

United Nations Children's Fund (in New York).

www.unicef.org

UNICRI

United Nations International Crime and Justice Research Institute (in Turin). The research arm of the UN in this field.

www.unicri.org

UNIDIR

United Nations Institute for Disarmament Research (in Geneva).

www.unidir.org

UNIDO

United Nations Industrial Development Organization. One of the **specialized agencies** with headquarters in Vienna.

www.unido.org

UNIFEM

United Nations Development Fund for Women (in New York).

www.unifem.undp.org

UNIFIL

(DPKO) United Nations Interim Force in Lebanon.

www.un.org/Depts/dpko/missions/unifil/

UNITAR

United Nations Institute for Training and Research (in Geneva). Aims to enhance the effectiveness of the UN and its Member States through appropriate training and research.

www.unitar.org

UNMEE

(DPKO) United Nations Mission in Ethiopia and Eritrea.

www.un.org/Depts/dpko/missions/unmee/

UNMIK

(DPKO) United Nations Interim Administration Mission in Kosovo.

www.unmikonline.org

UNMIL

(DPKO) United Nations Mission in Liberia.

www.un.org/Depts/dpko/missions/unmil/

UNMIS

(DPKO) United Nations Mission in the Sudan.

www.un.org/Depts/dpko/missions/unmis/

UNMISET

(DPKO) United Nations Mission of Support in East Timor.

www.unmiset.org

UNMOGIP

(DPKO) United Nations Military Observer Group in India and Pakistan, relating to the ceasefire in Kashmir.

www.un.org/Depts/dpko/missions/unmogip/

UNMOVIC

United Nations Monitoring, Verification and Inspection Commission. Mandated to verify Iraq's compliance with its obligation to be rid of weapons of mass destruction.

www.unmovic.org/

UNOCI

United Nations Operation in Côte d'Ivoire.

www.un.org/Depts/dpko/missions/unoci/

UNO

An incorrect abbreviation for the United Nations (organization). *ONU*, however, is correct in French and Spanish.

UNODC

UN Office for Drugs Control and Crime Prevention (in Vienna).

www.unodc.org

UNOG

United Nations Office at Geneva. Housed in the **Palais des Nations**. UNOG is the representative office of the **Secretary-General** at Geneva.

www.unog.ch

UNOMIG

(DPKO) United Nations Observer Mission in Georgia.

www.un.org/Depts/dpko/missions/unomig/

UNON

United Nations Office at Nairobi. UNON is the representative office of the **Secretary-General** at Nairobi.

www.unon.org

UNOPS

United Nations Office for Project Services.

www.unops.org

UNOSAT

A United Nations initiative to provide the humanitarian community with satellite imagery and Geographic Information Systems (GIS).

unosat.web.cern.ch/unosat/

UNOTIL

United Nations Office in Timor-Leste. A special political, follow-up mission to **UNMISET**.

www.unmiset.org

UNOV

United Nations Office at Vienna. UNOV is the representative office of the **Secretary-General** at Vienna.

www.unvienna.org/unov/index.html

UNPOB

United Nations Political Office in Bougainville.

UNRISD

United Nations Research Institute for Social Development (in Geneva).

www.unrisd.org

UNRWA

United Nations Relief and Works Agency for Palestine Refugees in the Near East, wih headquarters in Amman.

www.un.org/unrwa

UNSCEAR

United Nations Scientific Committee on the Effects of Atomic Radiation. A subsidiary body of the **GA**.

www.unscear.org

UNSCO

Office of the United Nations Special Coordinator for the Middle East.

www.un.org/unsco/

UNSECOORD

(UN Secretariat) Office of the United Nations Security Coordinator.

UNSSOD

Special Session(s) of **UNGA** on arms control and disarmament. UNSSOD1 was held in 1978, UNSSOD2 in 1982 and UNSSOD3 in 1988.

UNTSO

(DPKO) United Nations Truce Supervision Organization. Since 1949, supervises the armistice agreements between Israel and its Arab neighbours.

www.un.org/Depts/dpko/missions/untso

UNU

United Nations University (in Tokyo). Contributes to resolving pressing global problems through research and capacity building.

www.unu.edu

UNV

United Nations Volunteers programme serviced by a Secretariat in Bonn. Operates under overall administration of **UNDP** and funded by voluntary contributions.

www.unvolunteers.org

UPC

1. Universal Postal Congress. The five-yearly **General Conference** of **UPU**.
2. The Universal Postal Convention of 1875.

UPOV

International Union for the Protection of New Varieties of Plants. Although not a UN body, it works in very close cooperation with **WIPO**.

www.upov.int

UPU

Universal Postal Union. One of the **specialized agencies** with headquarters in Bern.

www.upu.int

Uruguay Round

(GATT) Multilateral trade negotiations which concluded in 1995. One of its results was the creation of the World Trade Organization (WTO). See **Marrakesh Accords**.

USG

Under **Secretary-General**. The third highest rank in the UN **Secretariat**. See **DSG**.

V

VDPA

(Human Rights) Vienna Declaration and Programme of Action. Adopted by the World Conference on Human Rights in 1993.

verbatim

Word-for-word, in full. How a statement is to be reproduced in the official **records** or **conference report** *(Latin)*.

verbatim records

(Only at some major conferences) Verbatim (i.e. full) records of all statements made in a conference. Prepared by the conference **secretariat**.

VIC

Vienna International Centre, where **UNOV**, **UNIDO**, **IAEA** and other organizations are located.

Vienna Convention

A number of Conventions have been signed in Vienna.
1. The one most frequently known by this title is the 1969 Convention on the Law of Treaties.

www.un.org/law/ilc/texts/treaties.htm

2. Also particularly relevant to the UN system is the 1975 Convention on the Representation of States in their Relations with International Organizations of Universal Character.

3. Shorthand for the Convention for the Protection of the Ozone Layer. Entered into force in 1985. Regular **COP** and **secretariat** in Montreal.

waiver

An agreed exemption, usually for a specified period, from an otherwise agreed obligation. Usually applies to one measure or one aspect of a measure within an agreement involving many measures. An example would be a temporary dispensation allowed to one party to a treaty to postpone implementation of one element of the treaty for a specified number of years.

Washington Consensus

(Informal) A set of economic policy themes which the Washington-based **international financial institutions** have advocated, sometimes as a pre-requisite for loans to developing countries.

Wassenaar Arrangement

A forum in which participating States discuss export controls on conventional weapons and dual use goods and technologies. It has a **Secretariat** in Vienna.

www.wassenaar.org

WCAR

World Conference Against Racism. The last conference took place in Durban in 2001.

WCMC

(UNEP) World Conservation Monitoring Centre (in Cambridge).

www.unep-wcmc.org/

WCO

World Customs Organization (in Brussels). An intergovernmental body dedicated to improving the effectiveness and efficiency of customs administration.

www.wcoomd.org

WCT

WIPO Copyright Treaty of 2002.

www.wipo.int/treaties/en/ip/wct/

weighted voting

A system in which the votes of different **delegations** are not equal but instead counted with reference to an agreed formula. In the **World Bank** Board of Directors, for example, the weighting reflects the number of shares held by the countries concerned.

WEOG

Western European and Others Group. An **electoral group** in **UNGA** and some other New York-based conferences. Includes Western and Central European Member States, as well as Australia, Canada, Israel (granted temporary membership in 2000), New Zealand and the United States. WEOG does not function as a **caucus group**.

Western Group

A **caucus group** composed of the members of **WEOG**, minus Israel and plus Japan, which meets in many conferences but does not usually adopt common positions or make **group statements**.

WFP

United Nations World Food Programme (in Rome).

www.wfp.org

WHA

World Health Assembly. The **General Conference** of the World Health Organization, held every two years.

177

WHC

Convention concerning the Protection of the World Cultural and Natural Heritage, adopted by UNESCO in 1972. Commonly referred to as the World Heritage Convention.

WHO

World Health Organization. One of the **specialized agencies** with headquarters in Geneva.

www.who.int

WHYCOS

(WMO) World Hydrological Cycle Observing System.

WIPO

World Intellectual Property Organization. One of the **specialized agencies** with headquarters in Geneva.

www.wipo.int

WMC

World Meteorological Congress. The **General Conference** of the **WMO**.

WMD

Weapons of mass destruction.

WMO

World Meteorological Organization. One of the **specialized agencies** with headquarters in Geneva.

www.wmo.org

Worker Delegate

(ILO) The member of a Member State **delegation** to the **International Labour Conference** who represents the workers of that State. Each delegation to this Conference consists of two delegates appointed by the Government and two others nominated in agreement with the most representative national organizations of employers and of workers respectively.

working group (WG)

A **sub-committee**, so-called to emphasize the point that it has a very specific and usually time-bound task.

working languages

The languages in which interventions may be made or texts may be circulated and considered. Although the UN has six official languages (Arabic, Chinese, English, French, Russian and Spanish), many organizations and conferences limit themselves to working in only two or three of these.

working paper (WP)

An informal paper for use in a conference. Their distribution is normally limited to participants in the conference. Usually a working paper is more substantive and less ephemeral than a **CRP** and less specific to a particular **delegation** than a **non-paper**.

working the corridors

(Informal) Engaging intensively in a large number of informal discussions, usually with a view to gathering support for a proposal.

World Bank

The **IBRD** and the **IDA**.

www.worldbank.org

World Bank Group

The **IBRD, IDA, IFC, MIGA** and **ICSID,** in Washington.

www.worldbank.org

World Meteorological Congress

(WMO) The **general conference** of the Organization.

WPPT

(WIPO) Performance and Phonograms Treaty of 2002.

www.wipo.org/treaties/en/ip/wppt/

WSSD

World Summit on Sustainable Development. Held in Johannesburg in 2002 with the aim of furthering the implementation of **Agenda 21**.

WSIS

World Summit on the Information Society. Convened in two parts (Geneva, 2003; and Tunis, 2005) with the aim to take action on Internet governance and bridging the digital divide.

www.itu.int/wsis

WTO

1. World Trade Organization, established by the **Marrakesh Accords**.

www.wto.org

2. The same initials are also sometimes (but not in this glossary) used for the World Tourism Organization, another of the **specialized agencies**.

WTO/OMT

World Tourism Organization/*Organisation Mondiale du Tourisme*. A **specialized agency** with headquarters in Madrid.

www.world-tourism.org

X - Y - Z

Zangger Committee

(NPT) A forum to assist **Parties** to the NPT to harmonize their export regimes, so as to fulfil their obligations under Art III.2 of the Treaty, especially as regards equipment.

www.zanggercommitee.org

ZNG

Zero Nominal Growth. A more extreme version of the **ZRG** policy.

ZRG

Zero Real Growth. A cap on the inflation-adjusted level of the budget of **specialized agencies** and programmes insisted upon by major donor countries.

UN DOCUMENT SYMBOLS

United Nations documentation can de identified by a combination of symbols indicating the principal organ/ subsidiary body issuing the document or to which the document was presented. Components of the symbols also refer to the session, the nature of the document and modifications to the text.

This list is not exhaustive.

A/
General Assembly

S/
Security Council

E/
Economic and Social Council

ST/
Secretariat

CAT/C/-
Committee against Torture

CRC/C/-
Committee on the Rights of the Child

CCPR/C/-
Human Rights Committee

CERD/C/-
Committee on the Elimination of Racial Discrimination

CEDAW/C/-
Committee on the Elimination of Discrimination against Women

DP/-
United Nations Development Programme

TD/-
United Nations Conference on Trade and Development

UNEP/-
United Nations Environment Programme

WFC/-
World Food Council

-/S-../..
Special Session

-/ES-../..
Emergency Special Session

-/CR/..
Credentials Committee

-/BUR/..
General Committee

-/AC. .../-
Ad hoc committee

-/C. .../-
Standing/permanent/main committee

-/CN. .../-
Commission

-/CONF. .../-
Conference

-/GC. .../-
Governing council

-/PC/. .../-
Preparatory committee

-/SC. .../-
Subcommittee

-/Sub. .../-
Subcommission

-/WG. .../-
Working group

-/CRP. ...
Conference room paper

-/INF/-
Information series)

-/L. ...
Limited distribution

-/NGO/-
Statements by non-governmental organizations

-/PET/-
Petitions

-/PRST/-
Statements by the President of the Security Council

-/PV. ...
Verbatim records of meetings

-/R. ...
Restricted distribution

-/RES/-
Resolution

-/SR. ...
Summary records of meetings

-/WP....
Working papers

-/Add....
Addendum

-/Amend. ...
Alteration, by decision of a competent authority, of a portion of an adopted formal text

-/Corr....
Corrigendum (which may not apply to all language versions)

-/Excerpt
Indicates the revise of an excerpt from a document when only petititon is required

-/Rev....
Revision (replacing texts previously issued)

-/Summary
Summarized version

-/-*
Reissuance of a document for technical reasons

▶ References

Berridge, G.R. and James, Alan. *A Dictionary of Diplomacy*. London: Palgrave Macmillian, 2003.

Boisard, M.A. and Chossudovsky, E.M., eds. *Multilateral Diplomacy: The United Nations System at Geneva—A Working Guide*. The Hague: Kluwer Law International, 1998.

Felthham, R. G. *Diplomatic Handbook* (7th Edition). London: Longman, 1998.

Kaufmann, Johann. *Conference Diplomacy* (3rd Revised Edition). London: Macmillian Press, 1996.

Ministry of Foreign Affairs and Trade. *United Nations Handbook 2003*. Wellington. Ministry of Foreign Affairs and Trade. 2003.

United Nations. *Basic Facts About the United Nations*. New York: United Nations Department of Public Information, 2004.

United Nations. *United Nations Treaty Collection, Treaty Reference Guide*.
untreaty.un.org/English/guide.asp

United Nations. *United Nations Documentation Research Guide*. New York: United Nations.
documents.un.org/

Walker, Ronald A. *Multilateral Conferences: Purposeful International Negotiation*. London: Palgrave Macmillian, 2004.